THE BROWNIE GUIDE HANDBOOK

Printed in Great Britain by
W. S. Cowell Ltd, at the Butter Market, Ipswich

THE
BROWNIE GUIDE
HANDBOOK

written by **Ailsa Brambleby**

illustrated by **Jennetta Vise**

published by **The Girl Guides Association**
17–19 Buckingham Palace Road
London SW1W 0PT

Price 80p

'It's fun to be a Brownie Guide!'

'We're glad you've come to
join us!'

'You want to know about Brownies?

'We are all from seven to ten years old and are going to be Guides later on. We make a special Brownie Promise and while we try to keep this Promise . . .'

GAMES

'We have fun out of doors'

'We keep fit'

STORIES

'We lend a hand'

VENT

4

'We make things'

'We are wide awake'

'We help at home'

'We do our best'

'We are friendly'

5

'You want to know why we are called Brownies?

Well, more than sixty years ago a man called Lord Baden-Powell had the wonderful ideas which started Scouts and Guides. Then younger girls wanted something, but the only name anyone could find for them was "Rosebuds".

'Of course no one liked that name and so they asked Lord Baden-Powell if he could think of another one. He thought of all the work the Rosebuds were doing and the fun they were having and suddenly remembered a story he had once heard.

'Here is the story in the way our Guider tells it to us:'

The Story of the Brownies
(Adapted from *The Brownies* by Mrs. Ewing)

'Once upon a time, many years ago, a poor man and his wife lived with their two children, Tommy and Betty, in a small cottage on the edge of a wood. The mother loved both the children but she was always having to find fault with them because they were lazy and forgetful and untidy.

'They used to rush about the place yelling and playing games, upsetting the furniture, breaking the crockery, spoiling their clothes and generally making themselves a nuisance.

6

'As long as they had a good time they never thought what a bother they were to other people.

'One evening, at the end of a particularly busy day, the mother sighed and said, "Oh dear, how different things were when we had a Brownie!"

' "What is a Brownie?" asked the children.

' "The Brownie," answered their mother, "was a creature who came to the house before anyone was up, and swept the hearth and lit the fire, drew the water and laid the breakfast table. He tidied the rooms, he weeded the garden, he cleaned the shoes and put the children's clothes away. He did every kind of useful work, but nobody ever saw him. He always slipped away before the people of the house got up, but he was the greatest blessing to everyone. Everyone was happy and the home was bright and clean."

' "My word, I wish *we* had a Brownie!" exclaimed Tommy. "He could do all our odd jobs for us."

' "Yes," agreed Betty, "and we should never have to tidy up after ourselves. Mother, do tell us how we can find a Brownie."

' "There's only one person who can tell you that," replied their mother, "and that's the wise brown owl in the woods; she knows all about the Brownies."

'So after dark the two children went out into the wood to seek the brown owl. Tommy led the way very bravely at first, but as the path got darker and darker in the silent woods he began to hang back and to feel sorry that he had started on the adventure.

'But Betty was eager to find out about the Brownie, and though she felt nervous, she would not allow herself to turn back, and she pushed on, leading her brother after her.

'Presently they heard the uncanny hoo-hooting of the owl among the trees. It sounded so weird that for a moment they stood still and felt inclined to turn and run back home.

'But again Betty thought of their chance of learning about the Brownie so she stood her ground, and hearing again the voice of the owl, which sounded more friendly as they grew accustomed to it, she went forward and presently came to the tree in whose branches the owl was sitting.

' "Mrs. Owl, Mrs. Owl, we have come to see you," she whispered.

' "Oo-hoo-hoo, I am glad to hear it. Climb up the tree, my dears, and come and sit by me on this branch."

8

'They did so, and, snuggled up closely against the soft, warm feathers of the bird, they told her their trouble; how they were always being bothered to work when they wanted to play, and how they had heard of the Brownies and wanted to get one to come and live in the house and do the odd jobs for them.

' "Oo-hoo-hoo, hoo-hoo-hoo-hoo!" chuckled the owl. "You see that pool down there. Go to the north side of it when the moon is bright and then turn round three times and say:
    "Twist me and turn me and show me the elf.
    I looked in the water and there saw . . ."

' "To get the finishing word of the rhyme look down into the water and there you will see the Brownie, and her name will fill in the rhyme that you want."

'So when the moon was up, Betty went to the pool and turned herself round three times and cried:

"Twist me and turn me and show me the elf.
I looked in the water and there saw . . ."

'But when she looked in the pool she saw nothing at all except her own reflection. So she went back to the owl and told her how she had seen no one there, except her own reflection in the water, when she had been hoping to find a Brownie who would come to the house and do all the work.

'Then the owl said: "Did you see no one whose name would make up the rhyme that I gave you?"

10

'Betty said: "No one."

'Mrs. Owl asked: "Whom did you see in the water?"

'Betty replied: "No one but myself."

'Then Mrs. Owl said: "Wouldn't the word 'myself'
make the rhyme?" And Betty thought of the rhyme:

"Twist me and turn me and show me the elf.
I looked in the water and there saw myself."

' "But I'm not a Brownie."

'Mrs. Owl replied: "No, but you can be one if you try.
You are strong and active. You could sweep the floor,
you are clever enough to lay a fire and light it; you could
fill the kettle and put it on to boil; you could tidy up the
room and lay the breakfast things; you could make your
bed and clean your shoes and fold up your clothes. You
could do all these things before anyone else was up, so
that when your mother and father came down they would
think that the Brownies had been at work in the house."

'Betty and Tommy said goodnight to the wise owl and
then went thoughtfully home.

'Next morning they slipped out of their beds early
before anyone was up. They cleaned up the place and
lit the fire, put the breakfast all ready, and crept quietly
back to their rooms, so that when their father and mother
came down, expecting to have to do all the work themselves, they were astonished to find everything already
done for them, and they thought the Brownies must have
been there.

'Day after day this went on, and the children had more
fun and happiness out of being helpful than they ever
had out of playing rowdy games or being lazy.

'It was only a long time afterwards that the parents
discovered that their own children were the Brownies who
had helped them and then they were even more pleased!'

'This story made Lord Baden-Powell think that "Brownies" was the right name. Brownies today are like Betty in the story and like the ones people used to believe in long ago. They try to think of other people – especially those in their own homes – and to help them every day. Sometimes they manage to do this secretly so that no one knows where the help has come from.'

'So that's why we're called Brownies.'

'And that's why some Packs have toadstools, as people once thought that the make-believe Brownies used to dance round them making the fairy rings which you can see in the country.'

'And that's why many Brownie Guiders are called "Brown Owl" after the wise owl in the woods.'

'And that's why some Brownies look in a Pack pool to see themselves just before they become real Brownies.'

'And that's why our groups or Sixes are called after different kinds of Brownies.'

'Maybe you'll join the Elves!'

'Or the Sprites!'

'Or the Ghillie Dhu!'

'Each Six has a Sixer, or Leader, and a Second to help her'

More About the Pack

'Every Pack has its own special secrets and signs, but some things are shared by all Packs.

'They are: The Motto, Song, Ring, Pow-wow Ring, Salute, Uniform, Law and Promise.'

The Brownie Guide Motto

Have you ever tried to feed a baby, take a pan off the stove, let the cat out, answer the telephone and pop an apple tart in the oven all at the same time?

Maybe not . . . but ever so many mothers have tried to. And they just haven't had enough hands.

Have you ever tried to write on a blackboard, work out a difficult sum, stop a paint pot from upsetting, catch a newt before it escapes and pull out someone's splinter all at the same time?

Maybe not . . . but ever so many school teachers have tried to.

And they just haven't had enough hands.

Have you ever tried to carry two shopping baskets and a handbag, find the right change, pick up a penny you have dropped, keep your dog out of a fight and give an ice-cream cornet to your small boy?

Maybe not . . . but ever so many shoppers have tried to. And they just haven't had enough hands.

In fact thousands of people every day need the help of an extra hand, so that is why the Brownie Motto is:

 LEND A HAND

Brownies keep their eyes open and try to lend their hands whenever they see they are needed. To save time they sometimes say or write 'L.A.H.' instead of the whole Motto.

The Brownie Guide Song

We're Brown - ie Guides, we're Brown - ie Guides, we're here to lend a hand. — To love our God and serve our Queen and help our homes and land. — We've Brown-ie friends, we've Brown-ie friends in North, South, East and West, — We're joined to-ge-ther in our wish to try to do our best.

We always sing this quickly and cheerfully.

18

The Brownie Guide Ring

'We sing the Song every week in our Brownie Ring. This is how we make the Ring:

'Our Guiders make a gate. We skip through this in our Sixes in turn, singing the tune to 'lah' and clapping until we are all through the gate and in a circle. Then the Sixers stand in front of their Sixes while we all sing the Song. At the end we salute, then the Sixers return to their places.

'While we are in the Ring, we often have Pack business such as collecting subscriptions, and notices.

'Sometimes we sing the Song again at the end, all holding hands.

'All Packs have something in the middle of the Ring to remind them that it is a BROWNIE Ring. This may be a toadstool, a Brownie pennant, a model of a pool or of a large World Badge.'

The Pow-wow Ring

Have you ever noticed that if you are telling anyone a secret you stand as near to her as you can?

In Brownies there are all kinds of secrets: special Good Turns to plan, Pack business to discuss and Ventures to work out (you will discover what these are later).

When dealing with important matters of this kind, Brownies hold a Pow-wow – that is they sit as near to each other as they can in a circle, so that everyone can hear and have a chance to give her ideas.

If you are lucky and have a Pack Leader to help you, she may tell you exciting news about Guides. (Pack Leader is a Guide from the Company which you will join later.)

The Brownie Guide Salute

'If you ever see anyone making this sign:
'You will know you are looking at

a Brownie Guide,

or a Guide,

or a Ranger Guide,

or a Guider,

'This is the Salute which we use to show we are all in the Guide family. The three fingers remind us that every member of the family has made a Promise which has three parts.

'Did you notice that everyone is smiling?

'There is always a smile with the Salute.

'Sometimes there is a Handshake as well – with the left hand.

'(Brownies, of course, still use the right hand with people who are not in the Guide family.)'

or a Commissioner.

Our Uniform

'Here's our uniform which we wear for the first time when we make our Promise.'

'Our ties are yellow. We wash and iron them often.'

'This is the Promise Badge: we wear it on the cross-over part of our ties.'

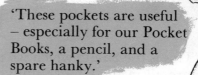

'These pockets are useful – especially for our Pocket Books, a pencil, and a spare hanky.'

'In winter we sometimes wear brown cardigans.'

'Sometimes we give our belts a special shine with shoe-polish.'

'Caps need a good brushing before Meetings. We always have our names in them.'

'The tape telling the name of our Pack is sewn on the left shoulder seam.'

'We wear our Six emblems on the left, below the end of the tie.'

'We try to have brown shoes and to polish them well.'

'We wear white or fawn socks (fawn or brown tights in winter).'

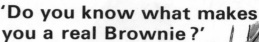

'Do you know what makes you a real Brownie?'

'Is it knowing the Brownie Story?
'That certainly tells you *about* Brownies.
'But knowing about them isn't the same as being one.'

'Is it wearing your uniform?
'That certainly makes you *look* like a Brownie.
'But your uniform is not *you*, but something outside you.'

'Is it meeting together with the Pack?
'That certainly makes you *feel* like a Brownie.
'But *feeling* is not the same as *being*.'

'Is it your Brownie Promise?'
'**YES!**'
'Because:
Anyone can tell you the Brownie Story.
Your mother may buy you your uniform.
Your Sixer may show you what to do at Pack Meetings.
But NO ONE can make YOUR Brownie Promise except YOU!

'Of course no one *has* to be a Brownie but if you really want to be one, you make an important Promise like everyone else in the Guide family.'

24

What is a Promise?

As you are seven years old or more you will understand the difference between ordinary words and a Promise.

Pretend you are looking after a very young child. You might say to her, 'Perhaps I will bring you a surprise to-morrow.' Then you might, or might not. But if you said,

'I *promise* I'll bring you a surprise tomorrow,' she would know that whatever happened and however difficult it might be, somehow or other you would produce the surprise.

Some promises are very short. You might easily say to your mother, 'Yes, I promise not to touch the television until it is mended.' Perhaps it would be mended within an hour's time then your promise would be finished. Your Brownie Promise will last the whole of your life, so you will want to be quite sure you understand it before you make it.

It is in three parts. The first is about:

GOD, OUR FATHER

25

God, Our Father

You know what it is to be a friend. Do you know what it is to be a very special friend – a real friend?

If you are a real friend to someone, you like to talk to her, to tell her about the things you have enjoyed and any exciting news you have.

You don't even mind telling her secret things about yourself . . . perhaps about some things that frighten you, or some you are sorry you have done . . . you may offer to help her and you know you can ask her to help you.

You give her presents, and you thank her for the ones she gives you.

You try to learn more about her and to find out the kind of things she likes you to do, and you try to do them. **Of course, you knew all this already but did you know that . . .**

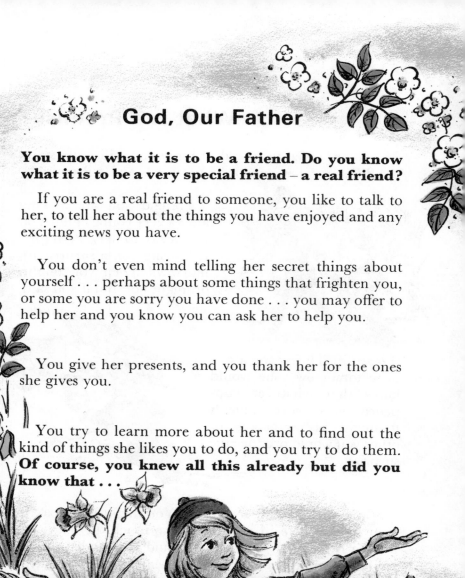

God would like every Brownie as a real friend

If you are a real friend to God, you talk to him (some people call it praying) telling him about the things which have made you happy and of any exciting plans you have made.

You may tell him about things that frighten you, and the things you are sorry you have done. He is glad if you offer to help him and he·is always willing to help you.

You will give him presents (you will have to work out how this is done!) and you will want to thank him for his presents to you . . . for your home, family, food, pets, birds, animals, trees, flowers – everything in the whole world that is good and beautiful.

You will learn more about him and find out the kind of things he would like you to do . . . and then you will try to do them!

If you want to be a Brownie you promise that you will try to be a real friend of God's; that is you will do your duty to God.
This is not easy, but every Brownie can try so the Promise begins:

I promise that I will do my best:
To do my duty to God,

27

The second part of our Promise is about:

Our Queen

All the kindest and best people in the world help others and serve them. Mothers help and serve their families; nurses, doctors, leaders of churches, and missionaries all help and serve the people in their care.

Our Queen, Her Majesty Queen Elizabeth II, on her twenty-first birthday, promised she would spend her whole life helping and serving us – all the people in the countries of which she is Sovereign. If you ever see her on television, hear about her on the radio, read the newspapers (or even run up to Buckingham Palace and have a look!), you will find how wonderfully she is carrying out this promise.

When she made this promise she asked us all to help her and to pray for her because she knew it was going to be a hard one to keep.

28

So Brownies promise that they will serve the Queen and join with her in trying to help our country and the people in it.

So the Promise grows:

I promise that I will do my best:
To do my duty to God,
To serve the Queen and help other people

This leads us to the third part of the Promise which is about:

OURSELVES

God helps the whole world.
The Queen serves all her people.
What do we ourselves do?
We try to help everyone we can – starting with those at home.
To help us to do this we have a special Brownie Guide Law, so the full Promise is:

I promise that I will do my best:
To do my duty to God,
To serve the Queen and help other people
**   and**
To keep the Brownie Guide Law.

The Brownie Guide Law

'Here is the Law:

A Brownie Guide thinks of others before herself and does a Good Turn every day.

'The two important words here are **THINKS** and **DOES**. 'In these pictures you can see a Brownie **THINKING** and **DOING**.'

THINKING   **DOING**

'All members of the Guide Family try to do one Good Turn every day. (Do you think this means they are not allowed to do *more* than one?)

'Most of us have our own special responsibilities at home, such as laying the breakfast table or taking the dog for a walk. This is our *job* so it does not count as a Good Turn.'

THE BROWNIE GUIDE PROMISE

1 promise that 1 will do my best:
To do my duty to God,
To serve the Queen
and help other people,
and
To keep the Brownie
Guide Law.

'So if you want to be a Brownie you need to:

'Hear or read The Story of the Brownies.

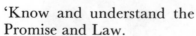

'Know how to wear your uniform.

'Know and understand the Promise and Law.

'After not less than 4 weeks, when you and your Guider know that you are ready, you will make the Promise and become a Brownie.'

The Brownie Promise Ceremony

All the Pack are glad to welcome new members so they all take part in the ceremony. I wonder what your Pack will do when your turn comes?

Perhaps they will make a Brownie archway for you to walk through till you reach your Guider and your Sixer who may be holding the Pack pennant.

Perhaps they will make a Brownie pool and decorate it. Then you could look in it as Betty did and see your reflection.

Perhaps they will stand in the Brownie Ring with the toadstool in the middle.

Perhaps they will make up something no other Pack has ever thought of.

Whatever is decided, these words, which are the same for all our Brownies, are said:

Your Guider will say:	'Do you know the Brownie Guide Law?'
You will reply:	'A Brownie Guide thinks of others before herself and does a Good Turn every day.'
Your Guider:	'Do you know that if you make the Promise, you must always do your best to keep it, and carry it out everywhere but especially at home?'
You:	'Yes.'
Your Guider:	'Will you make your Promise as a Brownie Guide?'
You (saluting):	'I promise that I will do my best: To do my duty to God, To serve the Queen and help other and [people To keep the Brownie Guide Law.'

Your Guider (pinning on your badge): 'I trust you to keep the Promise.'

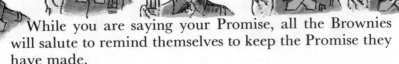

While you are saying your Promise, all the Brownies will salute to remind themselves to keep the Promise they have made.

Your Guider will then welcome you to the Brownie Pack and to the Guide Family all over the world.

34

'This is the Brownie Guide badge which you will wear when you become a real Brownie.'

'The badge as a whole shows that you have made your Promise.

'The Brownie Man shows that you are a full member of your Pack.

'The Trefoil shows that you belong to the Guide World Family.

The Pack Salute

'After the Promise Ceremony your Pack may decide to give you a Pack Salute. All the Brownies clap three times, once above their heads, once to the right and once to the left. With each clap they call out "Welcome". They then stand still and salute you, and you salute them.

'(Sometimes your Pack will use this salute to thank people or to praise them. Then they will say "Thank you" or "Well done" instead of "Welcome". If you are not already in a circle, your Guider will tell you how to run into one.)'

Now You are a Brownie!

Perhaps you would like to use this prayer asking God to help you to keep the Promise you have just made.

Dear Father in Heaven, we know we are your children; we want to serve you faithfully; we want to keep our Brownie Guide Promise. Help us to listen to your voice; help us to be willing and quick to do your work; help us to be friendly and loving; and help us to thank you every day for all your gifts to us. Amen.

Brownie Bells

Here is a kind of prayer which many Packs sing at the end of their meetings:

O Lord our God, Thy child-ren call,

Grant us thy peace, And bless us all.

Now you are a Brownie you will be taking a full part in the Pack – in Ventures, Journeys, Interest Badges, and in all kinds of games, ceremonies, acting, stories, and secrets. Now is the time to use your Brownie Pocket Book 2.

Pack Ventures

are kinds of Brownie Adventures – in which everyone has a part.

Pack Journeys

There are three of these. They are made up of all kinds of interesting things from which you can choose those you would like to do. On these Journeys you meet Challenges.

Interest Badges

There are about thirty of these badges, each connected with a special subject. You will hear about them all later on.

39

First of all we shall think about Ventures.

Pack Ventures can be:

Very Small   **or**   **Very Big**

**But
Everyone is Needed**

Here is the story of the Venture in the first picture.

Jean came to Pow-wow looking thoughtful . . . 'It's old Mrs. Green,' she said, 'who used to help Mum with the cleaning. I've just been to her cottage with a note, and she's not well enough to work any more, and her room looked all dull and she looked all miserable . . .'

'Let's do something for her,' suggested Mary, Jean's Sixer.

'What could *we* do?' asked Paula. 'We can't make her well.'

40

'No, but we could cheer her up' said Mary.

'Let's take her some flowers!' burst out Catherine.

'That will brighten her up and brighten up her room at the same time . . .'

And so the Pow-wow went on. In the end it was decided that everyone would bring one flower to the next meeting – not too big, not too small. The three Sixers promised to bring some greenery, a piece of silver foil and some ribbon while another Brownie, who had her Artist Badge, said she would decorate a card.

Then, after Pack Prayers in which they remembered Mrs. Green, it was time to go home.

As soon as the Brownies arrived the following week, the flowers were plunged into a jam jar and given a good drink. Then the Pack admired the card and planned what words should be written.

Finally they decided on:
         To Mrs. Green,
    We hope these flowers will cheer you up.
        With love from
          The Brownies.

But who should write it?

'Sally, of course!' shouted Mary, for although Sally was one of the youngest she was wonderfully neat.

Sally went to a quiet corner of the hut and practised writing the message on rough paper, then copied it neatly on to the card, while the others arranged the flowers.

Brownies ended ten minutes early that evening so that the Pack could all visit Mrs. Green. (Their Guider had warned her that she would have visitors!) She was very surprised to see so *many* visitors, and even more surprised when Jean stepped forward and gave her the flowers.

And there's no doubt about it, she was very delighted too!

This was a very small Venture, but it needed everyone to make it a success.

Now for the story of the second picture.

The church roof was falling to bits! One part was so bad that the birds used to pop in and out as if they were taking part in the services. No one minded that very much, but people *did* mind when the rain also began to pop in!

The Vicar (or Minister) decided to have a big fête in August to raise money. Would the Brownies help?

Now, it happened that there were several Brownies in the Pack who loved gardening and they begged their Guider to let them have a flower and vegetable stall. A large part of the next two meetings was spent in Pow-wow. It was discovered that some Brownies had special gardens of their own and would be allowed extra ground while working on this Venture. The Vicar said the Pack could have a big piece of his vegetable plot, and a good place for sweet peas was found by the Brownie hut. Three Scout brothers offered to help with some of the heavy digging. Some Brownies who were not quite such good growers arranged to collect gifts of flowers and fruit from people who had large gardens.

Then followed weeks of hard planning and hard work.

As the fête drew near there were posters to be made, the stall to be decorated, vegetables to scrub and flowers to arrange in buttonholes, posies and bunches. Then of course, there was the selling to do.

It was hard work . . . it was fun . . . it was a Brownie Venture! And now the rain can't find a way into *that* church!

Pack Ventures Can Be:

INDOORS

Making a Six Home

OUT OF DOORS

Making an outdoor den

AT ANY TIME OF THE YEAR

Saturday shopping for old people

AT A SPECIAL TIME OF THE YEAR

Easter presents in decorated baskets

HARD WORK

Clearing debris from an old garden

EASY FUN

Pack picnic

TO HELP YOUNGER PEOPLE

Party for a children's home

TO HELP OLDER PEOPLE

Giving an entertainment

DONE SEPARATELY

**Painting Christmas cards
for Pack friends**

DONE AS A GROUP

Painting a mural in Pack H.Q.

But Everyone is Needed

Can you

draw?

act?

sew?

make up stories?

think up good ideas?

use your hands?

dance?

imagine how other people feel?

46

If so, you will be needed in your Pack Ventures. You will be needed even more if you are a Good Clearer-Upper (or a G.C.U.).

I know a Brownie who is just like a vacuum cleaner! Whenever we have been doing an untidy job, she scurries round the room making the bits of paper, scraps of material, blobs of paste and dollops of plasticine just vanish! (And they vanish even more quickly when everyone helps her.)

The Venture Badge

People who are on expeditions, or voyages of discovery, or special work sometimes wear a badge to show that they are taking part. They may not all be doing the same things, but they are all in it, helping in their own way. If you are taking part in your Pack Venture you are entitled to wear the Venture Badge.

Brownie Journeys

Of course, not many Packs are on Ventures all the time: most people need a pause now and again to think up new ideas and to learn how to do new things which will help them in later Pack Ventures.

Because of this, each of you has some ventures or Journeys of her own which she can explore. On these Journeys you will meet all kinds of things which will help you to carry out your Promise, which are fun to do, and which will make you ready to take a bigger part in Pack Ventures.

The first Journey is called:

The Brownie Footpath

You remember how Betty in the story set out from the pool and returned to her home? In this Journey you pretend you are on a Footpath between the pool and the house – or your home. Along the path you will find all kinds of ways of carrying out your Promise.

Sometimes you will just take part but at four places you will meet a Challenge! You can see more about these on page 52.

Here is a picture of some Brownies on the Footpath.

These Brownies are all on different parts of the Journey, because it doesn't matter where you start or where you stop! It doesn't matter either how long you stay at one place.

On the Footpath you can wander where you will; you can stay for a while and enjoy yourself; you can meet and help someone and you can pause to learn something.

Do you remember the Brownies on page 4 who told you some of the things that Brownies do? Well, there is a chance to do all these things on this Journey and to meet Challenges in some of them too!

Brownies are Wide Awake

Look at the Brownies who are playing a game. They are all ready for their turns, thinking hard and playing well. When you have become more Wide Awake through taking part in a game using your eyes, ears, nose or fingers you may colour in the picture in your Pocket Book.

Brownies Keep Fit

One way to be Wide Awake is to keep fit. Ever so many people at home and at school help you to do this, but now that you are over seven years of age you will have begun to look after yourself.

The Challenge Learn how to look after one part of yourself such as your teeth, hair, nails or skin. Keep a chart to show how you have done this for a week. (Look in your Pocket Book.)

Brownies Do Their Best

One time when you can try to do your best is when things go wrong. Try to swallow the grumble and to put on a smile. Another way is to remember God and to ask him every day to help you in all you do and to keep your Promise. You can also ask him to help you to be kind, to be cheerful . . . and ever so many other things that we all need to be! When you feel you have tried to do your best in a new way, colour in the right Brownie in your Pocket Book.

Brownies Make Things

When you are on a Venture you may need to be able to paint or help to make a model so here is a chance to practise.

The Challenge Make something involving painting or modelling, working by yourself or with others.

Brownies are Friendly

Even if you decide to paint or model alone you will often join with your Six for all kinds of things and get to know them better. You will also want to find out about Brownies of other countries. You can meet some of these on page 74. When you have helped your Six to make something, or to think out an idea, or by taking part in a Six game, colour the Six on the Footpath in your Pocket Book.

Brownies Lend a Hand

The more friendly you are, the more chances to L.A.H. you will find. Look in your Pocket Book for some new ideas. Colour in when you have done a different Good Turn every day for a week.

Brownies Help at Home

Do you remember all the jobs Betty and Tommy found to do in their home? There are probably just as many in yours, and there is always plenty of cleaning to be done.

The Challenge Do a cleaning or tidying job such as cleaning brass, polishing furniture, clearing and stacking dishes, washing-up. Fill in the chart in your Pocket Book to show that you have done this over a period of time.

Brownies have fun out-of-doors

Of course Brownies don't spend all their time indoors, and when they are out they are Wide Awake and notice things.

The Challenge Make a collection of nature objects such as flowers, shells, leaves or cones, or make a weather chart. Arrange the specimens attractively and name them.

54

More About Challenges

There are four parts to a Challenge:

Choosing
You and your Guider do this together. Brownies always choose something they have never done before – or do the same thing in a different or more difficult way.

Learning
There is usually a right and wrong way to do things. It saves time to find the right way.

Practising

This can be fun – especially if you make up a game about it. It can be dull – see if singing at the same time helps. (You might notice whether the singing helps others too – or not!)

Using

When you have learned to do something and have practised it, try to find a new way of doing it as a Good Turn or in a Venture.

56

Some Hints on the Challenges

The Keep Fit Challenge

Teeth

What would you do if you sat down to eat and found the knives and forks were rough and sticky and covered with food from the last meal? You would wash them of course, because you would never dream of cutting up food with dirty tools.

Your teeth are tools and like to be kept so clean that they feel as smooth and shiny as a silver spoon. I'm sure you would not put the knives and forks and spoons in the drawer for the night if they were covered with onions, treacle, trifle and sausages, so why should your poor teeth be put to bed in that way?

Remember:

**'Teeth fresh and bright
Last thing at night.'**

They like to be cleaned after breakfast too, if possible, and do try to rinse them with clean water or to eat a piece of apple after other meals. Brush up and down as well as from side to side.

57

Hair

Have you noticed how beautiful mermaids are with their wonderful tails and hair? Maybe you don't particularly want to have a tail but everyone likes to have lovely hair. Why not follow the mermaid's example?

Keep your hair as clean as you can.

Let it have plenty of fresh air.

Brush and comb it free from tangles.

Arrange it to suit you.

Keep your brush and comb clean.

58

Nails

Your nails are rather like the garden lawn because they so often need cutting.

Of course, I'm not suggesting that you should use lawn-mowers to cut your nails – there are better things. Some Brownies use scissors and others use emery boards to keep them reasonably short so that they are easy to clean with a nail-brush, an orange stick, or a sharpened matchstick covered with a little cottonwool.

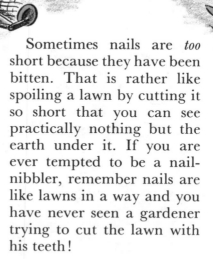

Sometimes nails are *too* short because they have been bitten. That is rather like spoiling a lawn by cutting it so short that you can see practically nothing but the earth under it. If you are ever tempted to be a nail-nibbler, remember nails are like lawns in a way and you have never seen a gardener trying to cut the lawn with his teeth!

59

Skin

Did you know that your skin is full of holes? Fortunately, these holes (or pores) are so tiny that there is no danger of your falling through them! Although they are so small they are very useful. Next time you become too hot look at your forehead in the mirror and see if the pores are doing their job. You will probably see tiny drops of water (called perspiration or sweat) which help to cool you and to clean your inside, because this moisture takes with it some of the waste your body does not need.

If you clean this waste away from all over your body – and any other kind of waste your skin may have collected from outside (dirt, dust and stickiness) your pores will be able to work properly. That's why you always feel extra wide awake and fresh when you have had a bath or washed well – it's like opening thousands of tiny windows all over your body.

You may like to think of other challenges to do with food, exercise, clothing, sleep, fresh air, or anything that will make you fitter.

60

The Model and Painting Challenge

Models

What difference is there between a Model and a Muddle?
Not much, unless you are very careful.
If you want to be a good Modeller rather than a bad
Muddler here are a few tips.

1. Collect all the things you think you may need and find
   a box to hold them. You may need one for your raw
   materials (such as fir cones, plasticine, nylons, match-
   boxes, pipe cleaners, cotton reels, and corks) and one
   for your tools (scissors, brushes, glue, etc.)

2. Find a box or lid for the model itself, to keep everything together.

3. Be a G.C.U.

You may find yourself working with other people on a
model but if you choose to be on your own here are a few
ideas.
    You could make:
        Something to do with Brownies of other countries.
        Something beautiful or interesting.
        A plaything for a young brother or sister.
        Part of a town or village.
        Animals for a zoo.
        A model garden on a plate or lid.
        A simple puppet.

If your model needs people or animals, you might make them out of pipe cleaners, papier mâché, plasticine, wire covered with old nylons, or dough made from flour, salt and water.

If your model needs houses, you could use all the small boxes you can find – not just match-boxes because the different shapes will make more interesting buildings. Some houses can be made from paper in this way:

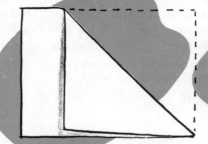

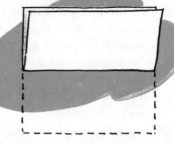

1. Make a square by folding over one corner of your paper and cutting off the spare part.

2. Fold the paper in half, making a strong crease.

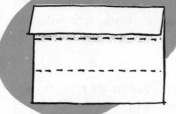

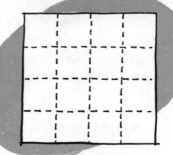

3. Open it and fold the two sides up to this crease so that you have three creases.

4. Repeat this, folding and creasing from the other two sides of the paper so that you have sixteen squares.

62

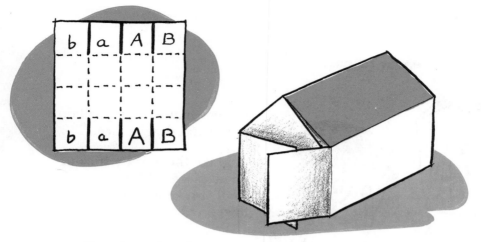

5. Cut along the six parts marked with dark lines. Slip 'a' over 'A' and 'b' half way over 'B'. Stick 'b' to 'B'. Then do the same at the other end of the house.

Painting

One idea would be to draw Brownies of the world, colour them correctly, stick them on cardboard and make them stand up.

Have you ever painted using natural paints? You rub on your colours rather than paint with them. Try rubbing a leaf on your paper and you will have a delicate shade of green. Yellow can be found in the middle of some flowers, black from poppy dust, red from red currants and so on.

One way to make a puppet

Cover a matchbox with plain paper and draw a face.

Make the hair by sticking on a piece of fur or some wool. Make a hole for your finger.

Place your hand on a piece of paper, tucking away your last two fingers. Draw round equally to make a pattern. Cut out two pieces of cloth to this shape and sew them together.

Now your puppet is ready to entertain your friends.

(If you enjoy this kind of Challenge you may like to work for the Artist or Craft Badge later on.)

64

The Cleaning Challenge

What's wrong here?

The important thing about cleaning is to make the dirt vanish, not just move to another place!

A Hint   To make sure the dirt doesn't move on to you. Put on an apron and roll up your sleeves.

Another Hint   To make sure the dirt doesn't move on to your home. Go into the garden or spread out a large newspaper.

A Polishing Job

Here are some tips for a good polish:

1. Use a small amount of polish and rub it into every corner.
2. Use a large amount of elbow grease, and rub the polish well out of every corner.
3. Carry on with a soft piece of cloth until you can see your reflection as clearly as Betty saw herself in the pool.
4. Be a G.C.U.

Clearing the Table and Stacking the Dishes

Find a tray just the right size for you.
Put the cutlery on one plate.
Scrape all the bits on to a plate. (If people are still at the table take the plates to the side of the room to do this.)
Put the saucers and plates in their own piles.
Do NOT put too much on the tray.

Which is quicker?
(and cheaper?)
Several journeys to
the sink like this?

OR   One big *trip* to the
sink like this?

Some people half fill stone jam jars or tins with hot water and put cutlery in them to soak.

Arrange the washing-up in some sort of pattern on the draining-board keeping cups, saucers, and everything else in their own piles. Find out which way suits your mother best.

Washing-up

There is a special order in washing-up just as there is in an important procession. Here it is:

Teapots march alone, and their leaves go wherever your mother usually puts them.

Hot water is dangerous to knife handles: knife blades are dangerous to tea-towels!

G.C.U's put everything away and deal with the tea-towels and sink before they go off duty.

There are other kinds of cleaning you might decide to do – anything from a pair of shoes to a spring clean of the house!

Whatever you choose:

    Keep yourself clean.

    Keep your surroundings clean.

    Use the right materials.

    Be a G.C.U.

(If you enjoy being a House Brownie, perhaps one day you might try the House Orderly Badge.)

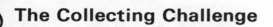

The Collecting Challenge

Brownies are rather like magpies as most of them like collecting things. They look around and decide to collect one special kind of thing such as differently-shaped leaves, flowers of the same colour, types of cones etc., while magpies just collect anything shiny from milk-tops to diamond rings – or the Queen's own jewels if they can get hold of them! Brownies make something beautiful or interesting out of their collection while the magpies just stuff theirs into the bottom of an untidy nest.

Arranging
The difficulty with collections is to keep them from moving about. Here are a few tips:

Flowers   Press them between blotting-paper or layers of newspaper then fix them in a book with tiny pieces of sticky tape . . . cover them with clear Fablon . . . make a small moss garden and gently push in your flowers. You can make neat labels for collections with cocktail sticks and gummed paper.

Shells   Arrange in a shallow box with cotton wool . . . stick on cardboard or in a box. You can buy tubes of very strong sticking material and you need use only a very little.

Leaves   These can be pressed like flowers . . . you can make scribble prints or spatter prints, and cut them out and make a leaf booklet from them. (Your Guider will tell you how to do this.)

68

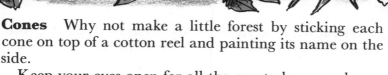

Cones Why not make a little forest by sticking each cone on top of a cotton reel and painting its name on the side.

Keep your eyes open for all the empty boxes and containers you can find and all kinds of ideas for your collections will jump into your head.

(This Challenge links with the Collector and Discoverer Badges.)

YOU WILL FIND MANY MORE IDEAS LIKE THESE IN YOUR OWN SPECIAL MAGAZINE, *THE BROWNIE.*

I am sure most of you will go for walks along the Footpath and do some of the Challenges. If you have done

something under each of the eight headings, you may wear this badge which shows the sign for a path which is used on maps.

Interest Badges

As Brownies are Wide Awake they are all interested in ever so many things, and like to learn and do more about them. You are lucky because in this book you can find out about thirty Interest Badges any of which you may tackle at any time you like. Before you start working for a badge, talk to your Guider about it.

You may find that you have to do most of the work by yourself if the rest of the Pack and the Guiders are very occupied with Ventures and Journeys, but perhaps you will be able to find someone at home or at school who will be able to give you some help. If you are good at looking up things for yourself, you will find all kinds of hints in special Badge Booklets which can be bought in Guide shops.

When you are quite ready to take a badge, your Guider will arrange for you to meet the tester.

Here are the badges which were mentioned on the Brownie Footpath.

 Artist (A Pencil)

1. Know the primary colours, and how to mix them to make other colours.
2. Using three of these colours make a pattern (which need not be a repeating one) by any method you like e.g. potato cut, home-made stick print, coloured paper. Suggest a suitable use for the design such as a book cover or printed scarf.
3. From your imagination make a picture using paint, crayon, ink, or other colouring material, but not felt-tipped pens.
4. Make two of the following:
    (*a*) An invitation for a Brownie event.
    (*b*) An illustrated prayer card for use in the Pack.
    (*c*) A book mark.
    (*d*) A greetings card.
    (*e*) A poster.

Water Rescuer (A Lifebelt on Water)

This badge will be tested on dry land and you may take it even if you cannot swim.

1. *Reaching*

   Know the way approved by the Royal Life Saving Society to rescue a person in the water:
   (*a*) by reaching with the hand
   (*b*) by reaching with the hand, using an assistant
   (*c*) by reaching with a pole or length of wood
   (*d*) by reaching with one article of clothing
   (*e*) by reaching with two articles of clothing tied together.

2. *Throwing*

   Know the way approved by the Royal Life Saving Society to rescue a person in the water:
   (*a*) by throwing a large ball or inflated ring or similar object to a person 5 metres away
   (*b*) by throwing an unweighted rope to a person 6 metres away
   (*c*) by throwing a weighted rope to a person 8 metres away.

Note: You must do this clause successfully 2 times out of 3.

3. Tell the tester how you could get help.
4. Tell the tester how you can be sure of your own safety.
5. Know what places could be dangerous near your home.

Note: If you have passed clause 5 and Stage 1 of the Royal Life Saving Society's Rescue Skills Scheme you can have your Brownie Water Rescuer Badge.

House Orderly (A Broom)

Help at home in the following ways and be ready to show or tell the tester what you have done or can do.

The tester will ask you to do two things at the test.

1. Clean two of the following:
   Window; basin; cupboard; brass; silver.
2. Tidy and dust your bedroom.
3. Wash your socks.
4. Make your own bed for a week.
5. Lay the table for dinner and wash up the dishes and cooking utensils.
6. Be able to do one of the following:
   (*a*) use a vacuum cleaner
   (*b*) defrost a refrigerator
   (*c*) use a washing machine
   (*d*) use an electric iron.

Collector (A Magnifying Glass)

1. Make an interesting, well-arranged collection of specimens in connection with your hobby or interest, e.g. stamps, postmarks, picture postcards, tea or cigarette cards, crests.
   The tester will judge your collection on number, variety and arrangement.
2. Be able to tell the tester something about your collection.
3. Tell the tester about a visit you have made to someone else's collection, or to a library, or art gallery, or museum, or stately home, or garden or zoo, and describe how the specimens there were displayed.

Discoverer (A Rabbit)

1. Observe seven living animals, and seven living plants. Be able to name and discover something of interest about each of them.

2. Following directions you have been given, take your tester to a spot unknown to you.

   To do this you may have to use a compass, follow signs on the ground, or look for growing trees or bushes or for landmarks. You may have to do any or more than one of these things.

   Keep your eyes wide open to notice things and to discover the way. The place you must find will not be more than 300 metres away.

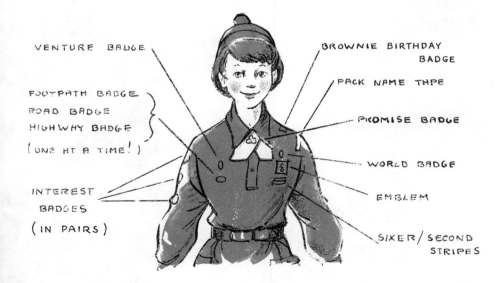

Some Brownies o

SWEDEN

FRANCE

Other Lands

NIGERIA

AUSTRALIA

More About Ventures

As you look at the Footpath, do any more ideas for Pack Ventures jump into your head? You will find that sometimes a Challenge can grow into a Venture. You may also find that while you are working on a Venture, you have accomplished a Challenge!

Models

You may have made a small house and garden. Perhaps other Brownies will add some shops, then a road, then one of you may want traffic. Before long you may have a model town. What about Road Safety? Could you put up some of the road signs and have some people crossing at the right places?

Perhaps you have made a dainty model garden in a tin lid using moss, tiny shells, berries, etc. It looks so beautiful that everyone wants to make one! Then someone suggests it would be a good idea to make three big ones, one in each Six, and then give them to someone who loves gardens but hasn't one of her own. Sometimes mothers will let Brownies have large old enamel plates or chipped serving dishes as a base for their gardens.

A Cleaning Job

Perhaps you have just learned how to polish brass. Then you hear that Mrs. Shaw who cleans the church vases and candlesticks is ill. What about a Pack Good Turn? Perhaps your Guider will ask you to teach the rest of the Pack how to make the brass sparkle. Then off to church with metal polish, dusters, aprons and newspapers will march the Brownie Brass Band! Perhaps your church could do with a little furniture polish too?

Making a Collection

A collection is the first step to an exhibition or a museum. Perhaps a few of the Brownies in your Pack could each make a different collection from somewhere nearby – the park, the sea shore, a piece of waste land. Other Brownies could paint pictures, make a simple model or plan, or write interesting accounts of visits to the place. Your artists could make posters or tickets . . . you could have

an open day and invite other Brownies and parents . . .
you could give the grown-ups tea . . . and orangeade to
the . . .

Gracious! Once Ventures start to grow they don't want
to stop. Keep a watch on yours at Pow-wow so that they
don't become too big.

Brownies Round the World

Here is another idea that never stops growing. Once you
begin to think of our family all over the world you wonder:

Could we all dress up as Brownies of different
countries?

Could we learn and perform some of their singing
games?

Could we choose one special country, make a model
of the Brownie and her surroundings, learn to cook a
meal she eats and to play a game she enjoys?

There are Brownies in nearly every country so you need
not run out of ideas for quite a long time!

Now is the time to have your Brownie Pocket Book 3.

The Brownie Birthday Badge

Everyone knows the date of her ordinary birthday, but do you know when your Brownie Birthday is? It is the date on which you made your Promise.

On your first Brownie Birthday you will be given a badge with a brown background. On your second birthday this will be exchanged for green, and on your third birthday, red. You wear it on your left shoulder.

Some Brownies like to say their Promise over again on their Birthdays, either at the Pack Meeting or when alone at home.

Are You a W.W.?

Just occasionally you may find that all the other Brownies in the Pack want to do a Venture which does not appeal to you. Perhaps they are going to clean part of the chapel – just the part you have always avoided because you happen to know that some very unattractive spiders live there; or they want to give an indoor play and you want to do some outdoor work. This is difficult, but it happens, and so it is as well to be prepared. If you are really trying to be a Brownie, you will know there is only one thing to do – to join in – and to join in willingly.

In other words be a Willing Worker or a W.W. You may need to be this even if the Pack has agreed to do the Venture you want, because you may find yourself landed with a dull part of it.

The Brownie Road

Here is another Journey for you to make.

The Brownie Footpath led you from the Pool to your
Home. Maybe one day you would like to try the Brownie

Road which leads from your Home to the village or small town. Along this road you will have the chance to take part in two things and to be faced with six Challenges.

This picture shows some Brownies doing a few of the things which might be done; you can probably think of many others.

TOY MAKER
BADGE

NEEDLEWORKER
BADGE

KNITTER
BADGE

CRAFT
BADGE

HANDCRAFTS

BROWNIES ARE WIDE AWAKE   At the General Store

Pretend that you are at the village General Store. Can you show that you are Wide Awake and that you use your head in doing something like the following?

The Challenge   Ring up from a public call-box, or carry a message perfectly, or shop reliably and politely, or pass an eye-and-memory test.

BROWNIES KEEP FIT   In the School Playground

The Challenge   Learn to do something new or to do it much better than before with a ball, or a rope, a hoop, etc., or do some form of balancing.

BROWNIES DO THEIR BEST

Choose for yourself one way in which you know you can do better. Here are two ideas.

1. Try to be quick-to-obey. For a week you try to do what your parents tell you just as quickly as a sailor or a nurse would obey orders.
2. Think of others in a special way by praying for different people every day for a week. (Those at home, at school, in hospital, etc.)

82

BROWNIES MAKE THINGS   At the Handcraft Shop

The Challenge   Make something for this shop by sewing, doing raffia work, knitting, weaving, etc.

BROWNIES ARE FRIENDLY   On the Village Green

Nowadays you often meet people from other countries when you are playing. You can fill in this part of the Road when you have learned a game or heard a Brownie story from abroad.

BROWNIES LEND A HAND   In the Brownie Hut

You have practised many ways of Lending A Hand but in this Challenge you are asked to find a new one.

The Challenge   Lend A Hand in the Pack by helping someone younger than yourself with some Brownie activity, or by making, washing or mending some Pack equipment, or by doing a special job for your Guider.

BROWNIES HELP AT HOME In your Home

On the Footpath you had the chance to learn how to do all kinds of cleaning and polishing. Now you can learn the care of clothes.

The Challenge   Wash, or iron, or mend clothes, or pack some in a suitcase or parcel.

BROWNIES HAVE FUN OUT-OF-DOORS In Your Garden

In this you have to look after something very carefully and help it to grow.

The Challenge   Care for any living thing over a period of time. You may grow a plant from seed or bulb, take care of a garden, look after a pet, or tadpoles, silkworms, etc.

Hints on the Brownie Road Challenges

Let us ask the Village people themselves for hints.

First we stop at the General Store. Here is what Mrs. MacNeil, the owner, has to say about being Wide Awake:

Carrying a Message

'You would be amazed at some of the messages I hear. The other day I was asked for "One pink egg with soft bristles and a dozen new-laid toothbrushes"! A few days later someone wanted "A jar of plum sausages and $\frac{1}{2}$ kilo of pork jam"! I soon sorted them out and then gave them this tip: "When anyone gives you a message always repeat it to her. This makes sure you have heard it correctly and helps you to remember it. If you receive a message over the phone, of course you must write it down." '

Using the Public Telephone

'The Guides are splendid when they come to phone as they have learned to Be Prepared, and they always have the right money so that I don't have to leave my customers to find change for them. Some of them have notes with them to remind them of what they have to say. A few of my customers rush into the booth, forget to read the directions and find themselves in a dreadful muddle. The careful ones read the directions each time – they don't gossip too long either. The polite ones that remember to say "Good morning" and "Thank you" to me look as if

they are being polite on the phone too. They are the kind of people who remember to give their names straight away, so that the person at the other end doesn't have to play a kind of guessing game.

'SO . . . Have the right money.
Know what you are going to say.
Read the directions.
Give your name.
Be brief.'

Being a Good Shopper

'This should be easy for Brownies as they learn to think of others before themselves. Just think of us behind the counter, then you'll be a good shopper. You will smile and say "Good morning" to us, and wait your turn. You will know what you have come to buy and won't keep changing your mind. You will have your money ready, check your change and pack your basket in a sensible way. You will walk out carefully, not knocking into people or things and will hold the door open for others. Of course good manners and good memories are just as important in self-service stores. A good shopper hasn't finished her job till she has handed over the goods – and the change! – to her mother and helped to put the things away.'

Being Observant

'The other day Clumsy Claude rushed into the shop. He knocked over a sack of potatoes, slipped on one of them and then sat on the rest. When he had cleared up he said, "Mum wants to know if the potatoes are in yet?" Nobody

would call *him* observant. Some of the Brownies who come to my shop are so wide awake that they not only remember what they have to buy, but when they reach home they can tell their mothers such things as that the apples are tenpence a $\frac{1}{2}$ kilo, the bacon looks rather too fat and the frozen peas have gone up again. Many of the Brownie games you play help you to become like this.'

In the Playground

Police Constable Evans is fit and strong and a very good athlete. Here are the tips he gives:

Ball Throwing
If you want to hit a target, look at it . . . if you don't look, you will probably still hit *something*.

Hold the ball lightly in the tips of your fingers – not as if it were fixed with glue to the palm of your hand.

If you throw with your right hand, stand with your left shoulder and foot forward. Now, why not try with the other hand?

Use your whole body . . . don't throw as if you were a one-armed lamp-post.

Ball Catching

If you want to catch a ball look at it . . . otherwise it may catch you!

Use your feet as well as your hands.

Balls can sting! But if, as soon as your hands have hold of the ball you move them the way it was going, it won't sting you so hard.

Ball Bouncing

You all know how to do this, and so can make up your own Challenge. Keep your eye on that ball!

Skipping

Don't be a Skimpy Skipper!

Here's one!

She can't help being all squeezed up because her rope is too short. Here's how real athletes find the right length. They stand straight, stretch their arms right out, and let out the rope until it touches their toes.

Be a Stretched-out Skipper!

Here's one!

When she is in the air, her arms, legs, knees, head, and back are all straight. Her chest is stretched as she is turning the rope backwards. She has springs in her knees, so gives a little bounce when she comes down again.

Perhaps you can make up a Skipping Challenge in which two Brownies turn the rope while the third skips.

There are many other things you can do with a rope as well as skip. Here's one:

Jumping the Blob

One Brownie has a piece of rope about three metres long with a bean bag fastened at the end. She swings it in a circle and the other Brownies jump over it. If they are not wide awake enough to jump in time – well, you can guess what happens!

High Jump and Long Jump are fun, but make sure you have grass or a thick mat to land on.

Balancing

Policemen and sailors some-times balance along a greasy pole, but Brownies generally make up their own balancing Challenges.

Here are some ideas to give you a start:

Perhaps you have a fallen tree near you?

Could you make a 'stepping stone' challenge using several tins?

Could you walk on two flower pots or tins, lifting them as you go along?

Has anyone in your Pack got some stilts?

What about hoops?

Could you make up a Challenge bringing in balls and hoops, or hoops and balancing, or skipping and balls? Of course you could try skipping across stepping stones while bowling a hoop with one hand and catching a ball with the other. . . . !

The last tip P.C. Evans gave was, 'Watch that those younger brothers and sisters of yours keep well away from the road when trying out these activities.'

(Ask your Guider to lend you the Athlete and Agility Badge Booklets. These will give you all kinds of ideas.)

The Handcraft Shop

Now we'll call on Miss Simkins who keeps the Handcraft shop for hints on sewing, knitting, weaving and raffia work.

'The easiest way to learn any of these,' says Miss Simkins, 'is to find someone to show you, but here is a start for you.'

Some General Advice

Practise on spare materials – not on those needed for your article.

Make something fairly simple to begin with.

Stop if you make a mistake and ask for help if necessary.

Keep your work wrapped up firmly or you may be sure that a kitten or small child will find it.

Start and finish off very firmly.

Press carefully under a damp cloth.

Sewing

Here are some of the things you might make: tray cloth, handkerchief, curtains for a puppet theatre, belt, hair-band, purse, pencil-case, apron, bag, bean-bag, book-cover, table-napkin, oven-gloves and face flannel.

It is best to use:
    Firm material.
    Largish needles.
    Embroidery silk or cotton.

The first thing is to be able to turn down a hem. Here's how to do it:

1. Make a Magic Measure. This is a piece of card about 1 cm wide and 4 cm long. Across it mark a line less than 1 cm from the end.

2. Turn down your material once until it is the size shown on your Measure, and pin it.

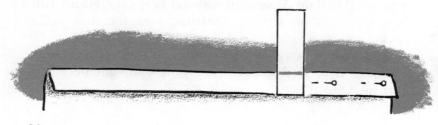

3. Repeat this to the end, and be sure to pin the corners firmly.
4. Tack with cotton then remove pins.
5. Add another line just above the first on your Magic Measure and start all over again!
6. Turn down a second hem till it is the size shown on your Measure and pin it. Repeat to the end.

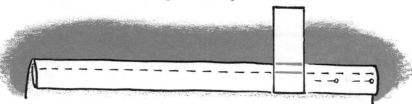

7. Tack, then remove pins and the first set of tacking. (This is a slow method, but it saves time in the end.)
8. Now you have a fine straight pathway on which to sew in a bright colour which will show up well.
9. You might start with a pretty tacking-stitch. If you use a knot, try to hide it. If you go over your first stitch twice, you will not need a knot.
10. Here are a few ways of adding to your stitches: you will be able to make up many others.

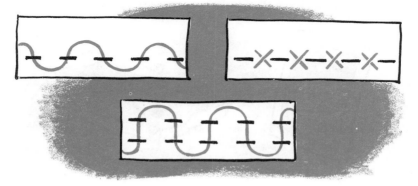

11. If you turn down the hems in this order you will find that the corners sit happily.

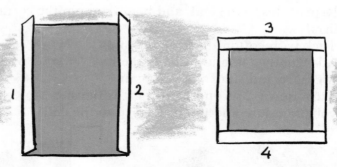

12. Once you can manage the four hems and over-sewing, you can make any of the things mentioned at the beginning.

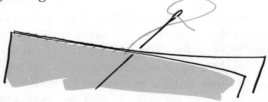

13. Keep the turned-down-hem side as the right side of your work as it adds to the pattern.
14. FINISH OFF WELL OR YOUR NEEDLEWORK WILL COLLAPSE!

Knitting

Here are some things you might make:

Squares for a baby's or dog's blanket, kettle-holders, spill holders to hang on walls, purses, tea-cosies, hot water bottle covers, dish cloths, bootees, mitts, pixie hoods, scarves, egg cosies, baby's clothes, doll's clothes, knitted toys.

Of course the first thing is to have some stitches to knit with so here is one way to produce them:

1.   Make a loop and slip it on a needle.

2.   Push second needle through the loop.

3.   Bring the wool between the needles.

4. Using the second needle, draw the wool through the loop.

5.   Using the first needle, slip the wool on so it makes a stitch by the loop.

D

95

You will find this DIFFICULT at first so you will need to try very hard.

At one moment you will feel that you haven't nearly enough fingers, and the next moment you will have too many – and they will all be thumbs!

Next you will need to make these stitches grow. Start as you did before, but instead of slipping the new stitch on the first needle, keep it on the second.

The stitches some people make change into work that looks as beautiful as lace and nearly as fine as a cobweb . . . but we shall be wise to keep to plain and purl at first!

Practise a plain piece of knitting until you are so good that you do not lose or gain any stitches.

To cast off

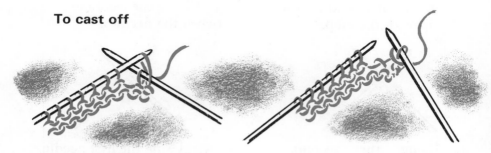

Knit two stitches, then with left-hand needle, pick up first stitch, lift it over the second one and off the needle.

96

Then try a square. If you can do this, you can make a dish-cloth.

With two squares you can make a kettle holder or a cover for a hot water bottle.

For more difficult articles look in a children's pattern book which you can buy at wool shops.

(If you can already knit, these hints are too simple for you and you should look in the Booklet on the Knitter Badge. See page 114 for details of this Badge.)

Weaving

Here are some things you might make:
Scarf, belt, bag, purse and table mat.

How to Make a Simple Loom

Find a strong wooden box or block of wood. Ask your father or brother to help you to knock in about ten nails

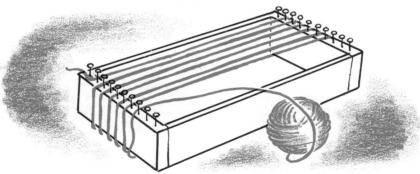

evenly at each end. Tie a piece of wool to one nail, then wind it between them and right round the box and tie off at the end.

With thinner wool, weave across the thicker wool by going over one piece and under the next. Be careful not to pull at the edges: the weaving easily loses its shape. By using different coloured wools, and by picking up a different number of strands, you can make interesting patterns.

When you have finished weaving the space between the nails, cut the wool below the box. These ends make a fringe.

Another kind of very simple loom can be made by cutting notches about ½ cm. apart in two sides of a strong piece of cardboard. Wind the wool right round the cardboard, going into all the notches. Weave on one side, then cut through the wool on the other side to make fringes.

Raffia Work

Here are some things you might make: mats, baskets, fruit bowls.

To make a simple mat, plait several long strands of raffia, gradually adding more raffia as you finish your first strands. Then coil your plait and stitch it together. I have

98

seen mats which are about four metres across made in this way, but perhaps you would do better to aim at ten centimetres at first!

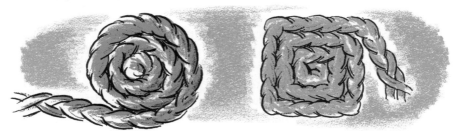

Simple bowls can be made in the same way.

Perhaps you can find someone who will show you how to wind and stitch raffia round rope as the Red Indians do. Their work is so good that they can carry water in their baskets.

Of course, if you prefer, you can do some crochet, tatting or embroidery.

(You will find ideas for some crafts in Needleworker, Knitter, Craft and Toymaker Badge Booklets.)

Helping in the Pack Meeting

The Village Brownie Guider tells us what she thinks about this.

She says, 'If you decide to help a younger Brownie with some Brownie activity, you will have to stop and think:
"Do I really know it myself?
Can I make it interesting?
Have we everything we need for it at Brownies or should I bring something from home?
Have I any ideas of my own about it?" '

Remember: to *help* a younger person to do something does not mean to *do* it for her.

Make, Wash or Mend Pack Equipment

The first thing to do is to find out what is needed. The most beautiful bean-bag in the world won't have a warm welcome if the Brownie cupboard is already oozing bean-bags by the dozen!

Whatever you plan, it is important to keep your work clean.

Thirdly, if any writing is needed practise first and make sure your writing is big enough.

Lastly, whatever happens, be RELIABLE, that is, have the equipment ready when you say you will.

Has your Pack plenty of balls?

Here is a way to make:

A Home-made Ball

Crumple a double sheet of newspaper into as smooth, round and tight a ball as you can.

Cut the leg off an old pair of tights and push the ball well into the toe (which you could dye a bright colour).

Twist the ball round.

Turn tights inside out so that the ball is covered for the second time.

Then continue to twist and turn inside out keeping the ball a good shape.

Smooth the remainder of the tights over the ball and stitch as flat as you can.

With brightly coloured silks or wools, sew a pattern over it, covering any rough edges.

A Special Job for Your Guider

No one can help you with this as no one knows what special job your Guider may have for you! Whatever it is:

Listen well to directions.

Try to do the job in the way your Guider would like.

Be a G.C.U.

101

In Your Home

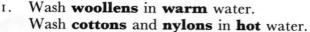

Care of Clothes

Here is a Brownie's mother to give you some tips:

1. Wash **woollens** in **warm** water.
   Wash **cottons** and **nylons** in **hot** water.
2. Wash **woollens** and **nylons** by **squeezing** gently.
   Wash **cottons,** especially dirty parts, by **rubbing**.
3. Keep **coloured** and **white** things **apart**.
4. After washing clothes need:
   two good rinses (warm water for woollies).
   two good shakes.
   two good pegs.

Try to discover the best way to hang out the clothes, remembering that you want the wind to blow right inside them.

Ironing

Ask your mother before you use the iron.

Make sure your hands are dry.

Iron small parts, such as collars and sleeves, before the big parts.

Use your common sense.

The best way to learn is to watch your mother then you will see the way she likes the clothes in your home to be ironed.

Have you ever washed and ironed your Brownie tie?

Folding Clothes

When folding clothes, try to make them into a rectangle; that is the shape of this book, only bigger. This means

that: dresses, coats and blouses change

From this   To this

Pyjama trousers and pants change

From this   To this

Socks change

From this   To this

Packing a Suitcase

Suitcases are rectangular so your clothes will fit in them neatly. We have borrowed some X-ray equipment so that you can see right into a well-packed suitcase.

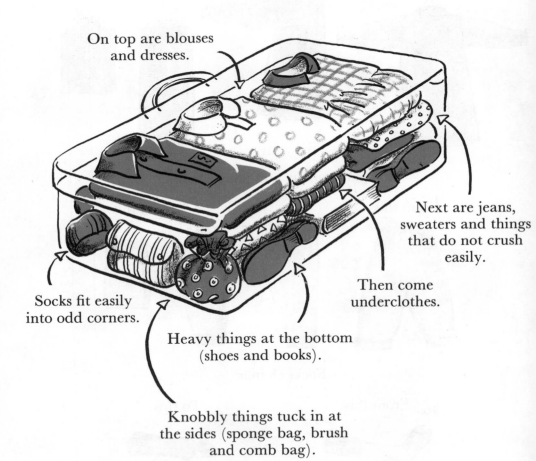

On top are blouses and dresses.

Next are jeans, sweaters and things that do not crush easily.

Socks fit easily into odd corners.

Then come underclothes.

Heavy things at the bottom (shoes and books).

Knobbly things tuck in at the sides (sponge bag, brush and comb bag).

Some people like a sandwich of tissue paper between the layers of packing.

If you can pack a suitcase well, you will be able to 'pack' your drawers tidily – but don't put your shoes in them, please!

Making a Parcel

One of the best ways of finding out how to pack a parcel is to have a try, so find an old cardigan, some paper and string, put them together and see what happens.

Did you find that the cardigan was too floppy to make a good shape?

Or did you find a piece of cardboard or a box to give it some backbone?

Was your paper too long or too short?

Or did you cut it just the right length so that it went round the garment well with enough to spare for a 'hem' to give extra strength?

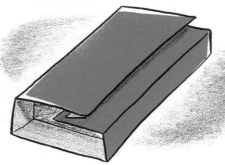

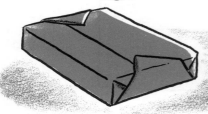

Was the paper too wide?
Or did you make it just wide enough for neat corners?

Did your 'wrapping-round' paper bounce up as you tried to do the corners?

Or did you fix it first with a slip knot?

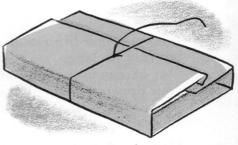

Did your first corner bounce up as you tried to do your second?

Or did you fix it with the string or sticky tape before you left it?

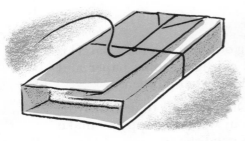

Did you finish off in a tangled blob of string?

Or did you find a neat knot for ending?

There are many slip knots. One of them is so good for parcels that it is called the 'Packer's Knot'.

Put the string under the parcel with the long end at the back.

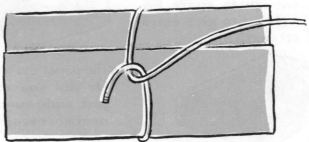

With the short end, make a figure of eight round the long one. To do this, put the short end behind the long one, then in front of itself and then behind itself. Then put the short end through the top loop of the eight and pull carefully.

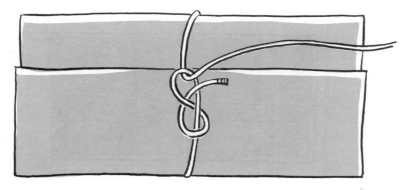

Here's a tip for the cross-over on the underneath of the parcel.

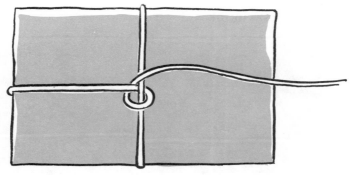

Put your loose end under the string, then over it, and under itself.

Here is a finishing knot.
Put your loose end over the fixed string twice, then finish
with two little loops over itself. This is called a round turn
and two half hitches. I expect you can guess which are the
half hitches.

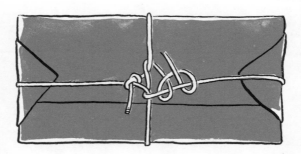

When you have finished, pluck the string as if you were
playing a guitar. Do you hear a good sharp twang? Good,
that means you have a fine tight parcel.
Remember to write the address and sender clearly on
both sides – in ink.

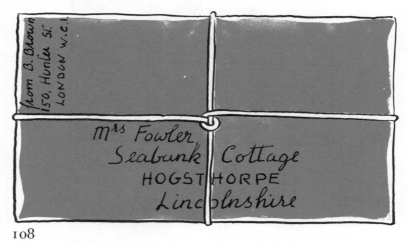

Caring for a Plant or Animal

Mr. O'Brien, who is a keen gardener and has many pets, gives us some advice. 'Remember that if you are looking after any living thing you need to think about it every day.

'Most living things need:
Food.
Drink.
Fresh air.
Light.

'Some need Friendship as well.

'Your vegetable marrow may not mind very much if you do not talk to it but your puppy certainly will.'

Ideas for Plants

There is no need to buy expensive seeds or bulbs.

Most people can find enough acorns, horse chestnuts, beech nuts, etc. to grow a mighty forest. (If you live a long way from trees of this kind there are many country Packs who would be very glad to pack up a parcel for you. Write to 'Packs' Pow-wow' in *The Brownie*.)

Many friends will be glad to let you collect seeds of nasturtium, marigold and other flowers from their gardens if you are careful.

If your father lets you dig up an old bulb, you will probably find that it has changed into two or three bulbs. This kind has to be grown out-of-doors. Bulbs for indoor growing have to be bought.

How to Grow a Bulb Indoors

If you want to make a home for tadpoles, silkworms, toads or earthworms, try to borrow a helpful book from school or the Public Library.

Always remember to ask your mother before you introduce a pet of any kind into your family: it is only fair to your mother and to the pet!

(You can find hints on this Challenge in the Booklets on Gardener and Animal Lover Badges.)

Brownies who have done something under each of the eight headings of the Brownie Road and have been successful in the six Challenges may wear this badge. It shows the sign for a road that is used on maps.

If you were wearing a Footpath badge, you will not need it any more and should return it to your Guider.

Some More Interest Badges

Here are the Badges mentioned on the Brownie Road:

 Agility (A Girl Balancing)

1. Show that you can stand, sit, walk, run, jump and land well.
2. Skip $\frac{1}{2}$ a minute without a break turning the rope backwards. Skip three fancy steps.
3. Show that you can perform a leap frog.
4. Balance walk along a narrow bench or on flower pots over a distance of 6 metres.
5. Join two of these actions into a sequence:
   (*a*) a forward and backward roll.
   (*b*) a shoulder stand.
   (*c*) a handstand against a support.

 Animal Lover (A Cat)

1. Look after your pet for at least three months, keeping a record of exercise, feeding, cleaning, etc.
2. Be able to tell the tester something of its life and habits, its daily diet and the care it needs.
3. Find out where and how you can obtain help for sick animals.
4. Describe to the tester the points you must consider before deciding what sort of pet to own.

Athlete (A Brownie Athlete)

1. Run 80 metres in 19·0 seconds.
2. Jump 80 cm. high.
3. Run, walk, or jog 1000 metres in 8 minutes. (You can do some of each.) You should do it on grass in a park or playing field, and only go on the road if there is nowhere else. Several Brownies should go together.
4. Run 25 metres skipping.
5. Throw a ball overarm 10 metres and catch it when thrown back.

Brownie Friendship (A Globe)

1. Choose six countries where there are Brownies and know one Brownie uniform and badge of each.
2. Know the flags of these six countries.
3. Tell the tester something which interests you about the Brownies in at least two of these countries.
4. Make an interesting collection (which you may arrange in a book if you wish) of views, national costumes, stamps, food pictures and labels, or similar things, from one of these countries.
5. Play a game and hear a story from another country and tell the tester about them.

Craft (A Spider's Web)

Do three of the following. Take two of them finished to the test and be ready to tell the tester how you made them and what you are going to do with them; and one of them unfinished so that you can show the tester how you are going to finish it.

(a) Make a picture, not less than 27 cm. by 37 cm., using a variety of materials, e.g. natural materials, cloth, felt, wool.

(b) Make a model of suitable materials, e.g. card, papier-mâché, clay.

(c) Make an article using material you have decorated yourself, with e.g. tie dying, embroidery, vegetable printing, stencilling.

(d) Weave a useful article not less than 25 cm. by 17 cm.

(e) Search for and find a small tree stump or branch or root resembling an animal or other attractive shape. Clean it by washing, allow it to dry, then remove all the bark and smooth with glasspaper. Mount the article on a base so that it will stand up, then varnish it.

(f) Make a flower arrangement to suit the season of the year, using not more than 7 flowers with as many leaves as you like. Know how to use a pin-holder, crumpled chicken wire or oasis and tell the tester which one you have used in your arrangement and why. Tell the tester how you can help cut flowers and leaves to last longer when picked.

(g) Make something using another craft of your own choice, e.g. origami, string work, puppetry.

Gardener (A Wheelbarrow)

1. Cultivate and keep tidy for at least four months a garden plot, window box, or boxes, pots, etc. on a greenhouse staging. Keep the tools used in good condition.
2. Grow two kinds of vegetables and two kinds of annual flowers from seed. Tend and train where necessary.
3. Transplant seedlings both into your garden plot (as in clause 1), and into a standard seed tray.
4. Gather some flowers for someone else (dried flowers permissible), and make an arrangement.
5. Explain to the tester how cut flowers and leaves should be looked after; at what stage flowers are picked and how to extend vase life if possible.

Knitter (A Ball of Wool and Knitting Needles)

You may knit or crochet
1. Choose your own pattern and, following the printed directions, make a garment using at least two different stitches.
2. Make something else of your own choice:
   gloves, mittens with thumbs, a shaped beret, a set of three fancy mats or something similar.

Needleworker (Scissors)

1. Know and use in the following clauses four of these stitches:
   chain, blanket, stem, cross, fly, running.
2. Make an article of your own choice, you can use a sewing machine if you wish.
3. Use a simple paper pattern to make a ball or similar article, and be prepared to show the tester how the pattern was placed on the fabric.

Toymaker (Noah's Ark)

To be a toymaker you should make, without any help, three of the following toys. They must be well made and finished and ready for use before you take them to the tester.

(a) A toy from materials which would otherwise be thrown away.

(b) A simple puppet using any suitable material. This could be a glove puppet, shadow puppet, a jointed puppet, two finger puppets, or something similar. Show how you would use it.

(c) Using cardboard or other strong material or matchboxes, *either* a set of dolls' furniture for yourself *or* a Brownie scene for your Six Home, the base of which must be 30 cm. by 23 cm.

(d) A toy of your own choice which is different from the other things you have made.

(e) A well-arranged, clean scrapbook as a special Good Turn for a grown-up or child in hospital.

Important Financial Information

How many pence in a pound?
Answer: one hundred.
How many pence in a Pack, if each week eighteen Brownies bring five pence each?
Answer: ninety.
This sounds quite a substantial sum, but just see all that it has to do.

Some Packs bring a little more and some a little less money, but the Pack belongs to *you* so *you* have to keep it going.

Perfect Pasting for Pernickety People

Often in your Ventures and Journeys you will need to paste something.

Challenge yourself with this:

Can you paste a picture on to a piece of card and finish with:

No paste on yourself.

None on the front of the picture.

None on the sides of the card.

None on the table.

It is possible but *only* if you are a **Perfect Paster.**

You need paste, brush, pencil and three sheets of newspaper bigger than the card.

1. Put picture face down on paper.
2. Hold it firmly in position with two fingers while you put on the paste thinly without touching the fingers.

3. Remove fingers. Steady picture with blunt edge of pencil and finish pasting.
4. Pick up picture by the edge and throw pasty paper on the floor. (Yes, I *know* it sounds untidy!)

5. Put picture carefully on card.
6. Use a clean piece of newspaper to press it.

7. Be a G.C.U.

If you have several things to paste, make a large tidy pile of newspaper, the pieces being bigger than the pictures to be pasted.

Remember to throw away the pasty paper and the 'presser' the moment you have finished with them, then you will always be working on a clean pile.

How are Your Ventures Going?

When you looked along the Brownie Road to the Village, did you find some new ideas for Ventures?

Think of those Brownies in the **School Playground**.

Why not have a special Keep Fit meeting or Venture? You could have Spring Sports and find out in each Six:

Who can run the fastest.
Who can jump the highest.
Who can balance the best.
Who can stand the straightest.
Who can stand still the longest.
Who can aim the best.

You can probably think of many more ideas. Perhaps you can make up Winter Sports in the same way.

In the Handcraft Shop

If several of you are good with your hands, could you help to care for a baby in a hospital or home for a short time by making her some clothes?

If nobody will lend you a baby, what about making an outfit for a large doll? She would be a wonderful companion for some lonely little girl.

Have you some good Washerwomen in the Pack?

Would it be possible:
>   for everyone to bring one used garment . . .
>   to wash, iron and fold the garments . . .
>   to pack them into outsize parcels . . .
>   then to ask your Minister or the Salvation Army to
>   pass them on to families who would be glad of them.

Are you good growers?

What about having a window box in your Pack meeting-place? If that went well, you might know of some dull building that could be cheered up in this way. Why could this count as 'Serving the Queen'?

Are you remembering to be a G.C.U. and a W.W.?

If you have plenty of Brownies who understand these initials, your Pack will be very welcome at:

Brownie Revels

A Revel is a kind of extra special picnic or party. It is special because, instead of just being with your Pack, you will meet other Packs and do all kinds of interesting and exciting things with them – including eating!

Remember

1. To take everything your Guider tells you to (perhaps macs, mugs, money and, of course, food).
2. To say 'Thank you'. How many times will it be needed?
3. To be friendly with the Brownies you don't know as well as with those you do.

Thousands of Packs manage to go to Revels each year and some extra lucky Brownies also go on Pack Holiday.

Pack Holidays

This is one of the best possible Ventures you can have!

You borrow a building – a house, school, church hall, or bungalow, and turn it into your Pack Home for about a week. You will need all the things you have learned on your Ventures and Journeys as you and your Guiders will manage everything yourselves! In addition to the fun you will have in cooking, cleaning and looking after your Brownie House you will have time for games, stories, exploring, picnics, expeditions, acting, and making things.

When you are on Pack Holiday you may wear a special brown short-sleeved dress, without a tie, or brown shorts or jeans with a yellow T-shirt.

After a Pack Holiday you may find you have done quite a number of the Challenges which come in the Brownie Journeys . . .

Now it is time to think of another of these Journeys. Pocket Book 4 will be of use to you.

The Brownie Highway

You leave your home once more, but instead of turning on to the Road which leads to the Village, you travel to places on the Brownie Highway which leads to the town.

There are still eight places to visit, and a **Challenge at every one**!

BROWNIES ARE WIDE AWAKE   At the Town Hall

If you work in a Town Hall you have to know what is going on; you have to be ready to welcome the Queen if she visits you; you must know the right days to fly the different flags and be able to tell people about your town.

The Challenge   Know and understand the first and last verses of the National Anthem; *or* know how the Union Flag is made up; *or* know the story of your town's coat-of-arms; *or* be able to describe an interesting place near your home.

BROWNIES KEEP FIT   At the Sports Centre

Good athletes and sportsmen train all parts of their bodies to obey them. Can you make your body do something new?

The Challenge   Make up for yourself a new Challenge connected with ball, rope or balancing etc.; *or* swim 18 metres (20 yards); *or* skate forwards and backwards in good style.

126

BROWNIES DO THEIR BEST   At your place of worship

Here is a chance to do your best for your place of worship, or for your Pack, to help you all to remember the first part of your Promise.

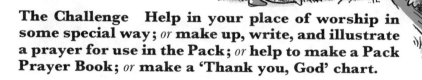

The Challenge   Help in your place of worship in some special way; *or* **make up, write, and illustrate a prayer for use in the Pack;** *or* **help to make a Pack Prayer Book;** *or* **make a 'Thank you, God' chart.**

BROWNIES MAKE THINGS   At the Concert Hall

Now you are going to have the chance to make things in a different way. You may need your heads, feet, or voices more than your hands as you are going to make entertainment for other people.

The Challenge   Take part in an entertainment by singing, acting, dancing, reciting, playing an instrument or working a puppet, either alone or with others; *or* **make up a story, poem, or playlet, and use it to give pleasure to someone.**

BROWNIES ARE FRIENDLY   At the Airport

Whenever you see an aeroplane you can be sure that in practically every country where it lands there will be Brownies.

The Challenge   Know the names of Brownies from five other countries and describe their uniforms and badges and be able to tell other Brownies about the Guides.

BROWNIES LEND A HAND   In the Hospital

Now you are going to have another chance to serve the Queen. It is worrying for her that so many of her subjects have accidents and that the doctors and nurses are overworked.

The Challenge **Know four ways of helping to keep
your own home safe;** *or* **be able to deal with clothes
on fire;** *or* **show that you can look after a small
child on a busy road;** *or* **know how to prevent simple
cuts, grazes and nose bleeds from becoming worse.**

BROWNIES HELP AT HOME In the home

We have already discovered
that there is always plenty of
cleaning and washing to be
done at home; there is also
plenty of cooking.

The Challenge **Make and serve a good cup of tea;**
or **make a salad or trifle;** *or* **fry a piece of bread with
egg, sausage or bacon;** *or* **make scones or cakes.**

BROWNIES HAVE FUN OUT-OF-DOORS   In the Park

It won't be long now before you are joining the Guide Company and going on hikes and all kinds of outdoor expeditions. Here is a chance for you to start to Be Prepared to be useful out-of-doors.

The Challenge   Set a compass and know 8 points; *or* **make a simple map showing the nearest police station, chemist's shop, hospital, telephone, post office, garage, and filling station, to your home or Pack meeting-place;** *or* **signal messages to someone who is out of hearing;** *or* **know how to use a bus time-table.**

Hints on the Brownie Highway Challenges

At the Town Hall

The National Anthem

Here are the words of the first and last verses:

God save our gracious Queen,
Long live our noble Queen,
    God save the Queen!
Send her victorious,
Happy and glorious,
Long to reign over us,
    God save the Queen!

Thy choicest gifts in store
On her be pleased to pour,
    Long may she reign.
May she defend our laws,
And ever give us cause
To sing with heart and voice,
    God save the Queen!

This is a kind of prayer in which we ask God to bless our Queen. We stand to attention when we sing or hear it and think of the meaning of the words. It was written over a hundred years ago so some of the words may sound old-fashioned to us. See if you can pick out the ones in which we are asking God:

to let her be our Queen for many years
to give her goodness, wisdom and happiness
to help her to be a good Queen
to protect her from harm.

Did you know that a really 'gracious' person is one who thinks of others before herself? What do you think 'noble' means?

What would you include if you were asked to make up a third verse? Why not have a try?

The Union Flag

When you are a Guide you will often look at the Union Flag and salute while singing the National Anthem. This is because this flag reminds us of our Queen and our country.

You can see that it is made up of three crosses. They stand for three men who were so splendid that we still remember them although they have been dead for hundreds and hundreds of years.

1. **On 17th March** you will be able to discover which is St. Patrick's flag. He spent years of his life telling the people of Ireland about God. His early life was very exciting for he was kidnapped as a boy but later managed to escape.

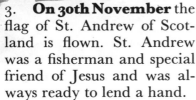

2. **On 23rd April** you will discover which is the Cross of St. George of England. Stories about him tell us that he was a soldier who always tried to obey God; that he once saved a princess very bravely, and that he was always ready to help other people.

3. **On 30th November** the flag of St. Andrew of Scotland is flown. St. Andrew was a fisherman and special friend of Jesus and was always ready to lend a hand.

On 1st March we remember another fine man, St. David of Wales. Wherever he went he comforted and helped people. He did this sometimes by singing to them for he had a most wonderful voice.

133

On St. Patrick's day you will often see Irish people wearing shamrock. What might the English, Scottish and Welsh people wear on their national day?

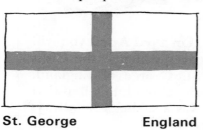

St. George   **England**

St. Andrew   **Scotland**

St. Patrick   **Ireland**

The Union Flag

A union is a joining together. The crosses are joined to make one flag, the Union Flag for the United Kingdom of England, Scotland, Northern Ireland and Wales.

There is a right way and a wrong way to fly this flag. Can you find out what they are?

134

A coat of arms is a kind of badge which often tells something of the story of the person or place to which it belongs. Ask the Librarian at your public library to help you to find a book which tells you about the badge of your town. Perhaps you could draw or paint it on a book cover. When you are away on holiday you could look out for other coats-of-arms and copy them into the book. Counties and countries also have their own badges . . . and these have a place in Brownie Packs. Can you find any in your Pack?

Interesting Places

Once you start looking for them you will find it hard to stop! You may choose a very small cottage or an enormous cathedral; a place where rare wild plants grow or a beautifully cultivated park; an old dark well, or a modern flood-lit fountain. Here again you will be able to find help in the library, but no matter how much you read always try to discover something for yourself that no one else has found.

(You may be interested in the Booklover Badge after all this reading!)

At the Sports Centre

Ball Throwing

Can you throw over-arm as
well as under? Boys are usually much better at this than
girls so watch how they do it.
If your ball does not travel
far enough, try throwing it
higher – perhaps over a rope
held by two people.

Swimming

Eighteen metres looks a long way at first, but remember,
everyone can swim *one* metre! Just drop yourself gently on
the water and push hard with your foot and you've done
it. The next time, push the water away with your arms
and perhaps you will do *two* metres. Then multiply that by
nine and there you are! Sometimes it helps if you practise
the arm and leg movements while lying on your tummy
on a chair.

1

2

3

Skipping

Now is the time to try some fancy steps. Those you make up yourself are the most interesting. What happens when you cross your hands or your feet? You trip up? Well, maybe at first, but you will soon succeed if you practise.

Why not work at ball-throwing and skipping with a friend and try moving to music. Together you might be able to make up a dance.

Skating

When skating:
Push from the side of the blade – not the toe.
Keep your weight slightly forward – but stand upright.
Look ahead – not at your feet.
Bend your knees well.

When learning to skate *backwards* concentrate on the outside edges; bringing legs close together when changing feet. The pattern you make on the ice should be

like this:

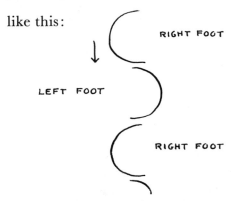

RIGHT FOOT

LEFT FOOT

RIGHT FOOT

When skating *back*wards, please do remember the *front* part of the Brownie Law!

Your Place of Worship

Make up a Prayer

Here is one way to start. Decide whether you will write a 'thanking', an 'asking', or a 'praising' prayer, or one for forgiveness. Then make a list of the five or six chief things you want to include and make a sentence about each. You can probably think of many more but it is better to keep to a few special ones. You may decide to have a refrain such as 'We thank Thee, O God' or 'Please hear our prayer'. Then one of the Pack could read the sentence and the rest of you could say the refrain together.

You could then write the prayer on firm card and illustrate it with some of the things you have mentioned in the prayer. After all your hard work it would be worth while to cover the card with transparent plastic or polythene to keep it clean and make it last longer.

Pack Prayer Book

It is often better for each Brownie to write a prayer on loose paper and then stick it in rather than to write straight in the book. Your own illustrations are usually more interesting than printed ones, but sometimes very suitable and beautiful cards can be found. Perhaps you will help to make and decorate a cover for the book. Someone in the Pack may know how to make paste papers or potato prints.

138

A 'Thank You' Chart

This chart gives everyone in the Pack the chance to thank God for something, and as God has given us so many things you will need to make it a big chart! At the top you need the words:

 THANK YOU, GOD

You might like to have a drawing under this heading, or a design or illustration all round the chart. Then rule lines, about half an inch apart and a margin on the right-hand side. Each Brownie has at least one line in which she writes:

I THANK GOD FOR . . .

putting in something that is special for her. In the margin she writes her initials.

You could make another kind of chart by sticking on a matchbox for each Six. If you did this you would not need the lines, as each Brownie would write her 'Thank you' on a piece of paper and post it in her Six's box.

Service to your Place of Worship

You will have to plan this carefully with your Guider and the leader of your church. Remember that if you take on regular work for a period of time it should *really* be regular!

The Concert Hall

When you are entertaining people you have 'to think of others before yourself', in two ways.

First of all, think of your audience: try to choose something which they will enjoy and rehearse it well.

Then you have to think of whom you are meant to be, or about whom you are reciting or singing. You have to try to turn into that person – every part of you – your thoughts, face, voice and all your movements.

There are many badges linked with this Challenge and you will find help in the Booklets on Dancer, Jester, Musician, Music Lover, and Writer badges.

The Airport

Did you know that there are Brownies in over ninety different countries? All of them have made a Promise and they all Lend A Hand, and all have some kind of Ventures and Challenges. It is fun to keep your eyes open when reading *The Brownie* and to make a list of any things these Brownies do which are different from ours. Could *you* make something useful out of a banana leaf, I wonder?

This Challenge is a good one to work for near Thinking Day (see page 167) and you will find help with it in the Booklet on Brownie Friendship badge and in *Brownies of the World* painting books.

140

How are you going to find out about your own Guide Company in order to tell other Brownies about it?

Well, first, let me tell you, you won't find out ALL about it, however hard you try for there will be some surprises and secrets just as there are in the Pack. Here are a few ways of gathering information:

1. Ask Pack Leader
How many Patrols there are and what are their names?
Where does the Company meet in summer?
Have they Patrol dens?
What is the most exciting thing they have ever done?

2. Ask your Guider if you may visit the Company
It is a great honour to be allowed to attend a Company meeting before you are a Guide. Remember your Salute and watch out for the sign which the Company uses for 'quiet'. You will have to be very wide awake to notice it as quickly as the Guides! Of course you will remember to thank the Guider and Patrol Leaders at the end of the meeting.

Some things to find out

See if you can discover them yourself when you are at the meeting.

What does a Guide have to do before she receives her Promise Badge?

What Enterprises have the Patrols done lately?

What happens at Patrol Leaders' Council?

Is there a Guide wearing an Eight Point Badge? a Collective Emblem? a Service Flash?

What Company Service Project have they done this year?

What happened at the last camp?

Has any Patrol a P.I.P.?

3.   See if by any chance you can wanglé a day in camp
This may *sound* impossible but have a try. If you are successful, keep your eyes open for any jobs with which you can help.

4. Read *Today's Guide*
You can probably borrow a copy from a friend, but now that you are nearly ready to move on, why not start to take this instead of *The Brownie*?

The Hospital

Can you think of anything that is better than helping people when they are hurt?

There is one thing, and that is doing something to prevent them from getting hurt.

It is very helpful if you know how to treat simple injuries and how to ring up the doctor or ambulance: it is even more helpful if you keep yourself so wide awake that you prevent accidents from happening.

Here are some things which might cause accidents in your home – especially if there is anyone very old or very young in it:

Toys on the stairs or floor; plastic bags; hot pans on the kitchen stove; tea-pots on the table; knives; scissors; bottles of medicine; doors on windy days; small rugs.

Think of the accidents that might happen and think of how you would deal with them, then check your ideas by looking in the Safety in the Home Badge Booklet, or by consulting your Guider.

Clothes on Fire

Many Brownies have saved people from being badly burnt because they have known what to do when clothes catch fire.

1. Wrap a coat or rug round the person, calling for help at the same time.

2. Push her to the ground.

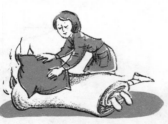 

3. Roll her over and beat out the flames.

4. Make her comfortable.

5. Fetch a grown up *at once*.

If you have nothing to cover the burning clothes, stop the patient from moving, push her on the ground and roll her over and over.

144

Looking after a Child in the Road

No two roads are alike so you will have to think out this Challenge in relation to those near your home.

Here are three tips and three questions:

Hold the child's hand.

Cross at the special places provided.

Look all round for traffic and listen before crossing.

Now for the questions:
Should you walk or run across the road?
If the child has a ball, who should carry it?
When on the pavement, which side of you should the child walk?

Simple First Aid

Cuts and Grazes

Cleanliness is the greatest help in these:
1. Clean your hands – with soap and water if possible.
2. Clean the wound – with water and rag or cotton wool.
3. Keep the wound clean – cover with a dressing which can be an adhesive dressing, clean handkerchief, or rag.

You may need a bandage to hold the dressing in place. You will find how to apply this in the Booklet on First Aider Badge.

The Reef Knot

All First Aiders should be able to tie this useful knot as it lies flat and does not dig into the patient.

This is the way to tie the reef knot using a black rope and a white one.

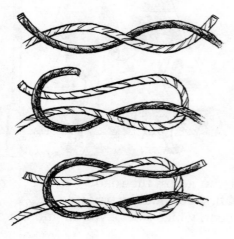

1. The black end goes over the white, under it, then over again.

2. Then the two ends face each other and the black goes over, under and over again.

3. This makes the reef knot.

A Tip about Adhesive Dressings

Sometimes this does not stay for long on a bouncy finger or wriggly knee. Try making a slit on each end. Separate the ends when you put on the adhesive dressing and you will find that it grips well.

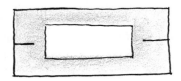

Nose bleed

1. Tell the patient to sit with her head tipped slightly forward.

2. Pinch her nose firmly on the soft lower part.

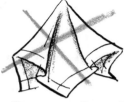

3. Do not let the patient blow her nose.

4. Report to an adult.

At Home

A good cup of tea

Do you know the main difference between a cup of tea and a *good* cup of tea?

The answer is boiling water.

When you have warmed the pot and put in about one teaspoonful of tea (or a little more) for each person, very carefully pour on *boiling* water. It must be really bubbling – and yet it must not have bubbled for too long or the tea will have a 'flat' taste . . . stir the tea and do not pour it for about five minutes.

Most people enjoy their tea more if it is well served.

Make sure you have a clean traycloth.

See that everything you need is on the tray.

(Remember Safety in the Home and be sure that no small children or pets are running round you when you are handling the kettle.)

Salad or Trifle

There is not much cooking to be done here, but a great deal of arranging to make the dish look really attractive.

For salads:

Everything must be very well washed.

Beetroot colours other vegetables so it is often better in a dish by itself.

Helpful hints on this Challenge can be found in the Cook Badge Booklet, but here is a recipe which you may like to try.

Fairy Cakes

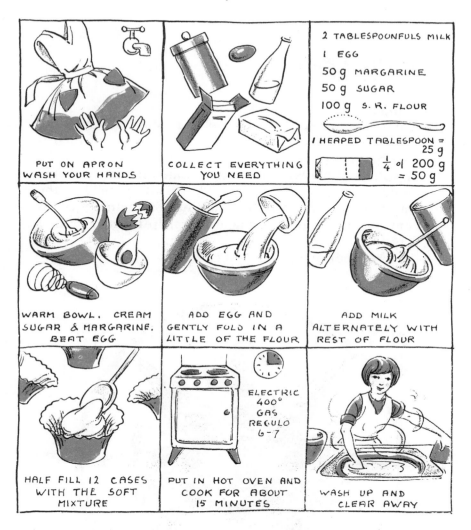

PUT ON APRON
WASH YOUR HANDS

COLLECT EVERYTHING
YOU NEED

2 TABLESPOONFULS MILK
1 EGG
50 g MARGARINE
50 g SUGAR
100 g S.R. FLOUR
1 HEAPED TABLESPOON = 25 g
$\frac{1}{4}$ of 200 g = 50 g

WARM BOWL. CREAM
SUGAR & MARGARINE.
BEAT EGG

ADD EGG AND
GENTLY FOLD IN A
LITTLE OF THE FLOUR

ADD MILK
ALTERNATELY WITH
REST OF FLOUR

HALF FILL 12 CASES
WITH THE SOFT
MIXTURE

PUT IN HOT OVEN AND
COOK FOR ABOUT
15 MINUTES

ELECTRIC
400°
GAS
REGULO
6-7

WASH UP AND
CLEAR AWAY

Which two pictures here apply to *all* cooking?

If you can make a good cup of tea and if you can bake a good batch of fairy cakes, you will be ready to think about the Hostess Badge. (See page 159.)

In the Park

Compass

Have you ever read the kind of fairy story in which the hero sets out alone on a hazardous journey and then is lost? Suddenly a strange creature – a witch, fairy, or toad – appears and makes him a gift of something like a magic pebble or feather. This, he is told, will always tell him the way to go. Guides and Brownies have something just as convenient and just as magical to help them find their way.

Here is our magic 'gift' – a compass.

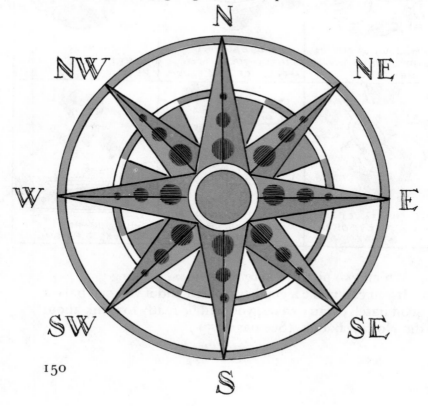

Wherever you have your compass – at home or in the street, at Pack Meeting or at school, on a picnic or on Revels – its needle will swing to and fro in an excited way until it finds the direction in which it wants to point. This direction is always the same – to the North part of the world.

So, with a compass you can always find where North is. From that you can work out South, East, and West, and then the points between them.

Because of this, sailors, soldiers, airmen, Guides, Brownies and other people who like travelling and exploring learn how to use the compass to help them to find their way.

Try to buy or borrow a compass and find out which way your bedroom faces, your main road runs, etc.

Even without a compass you can often find North. The sun is a help. Do you know where it rises and sets?

Maps

When you are a Guide you will learn how to follow maps which are full of footpaths, roads, and highways all crossing over each other. Your map, however, will be much more simple. Put your home or Brownie head-quarters in the middle of the page, draw in and name the roads. You will have to use a simple scale such as $2\frac{1}{2}$ cms for every quarter of a mile. Then fill in the places.

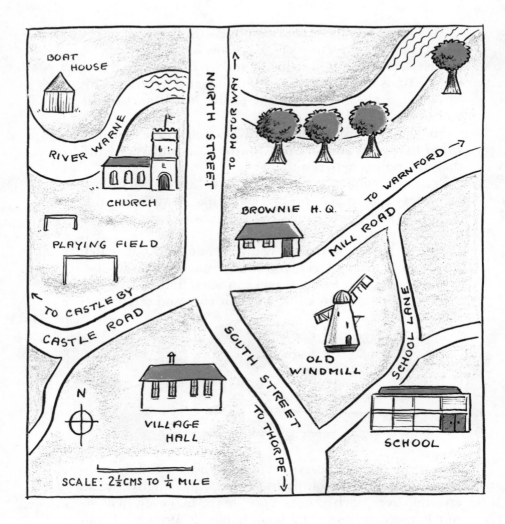

Can you put in North? You can also put in the names of the places to which the main roads lead, and any interesting or important buildings.

Signalling

Many Brownies and Guides like to send messages without talking. Sailors, soldiers and explorers have often saved lives by being able to do this. Semaphore is fun as you can signal it with flags or with your arms or you can write it.

Hints

Keep your body straight and your feet slightly apart.
Never move from one letter till you are sure of the position of the next.
Bring your arms down in front of you at the end of each word.
Signal slowly and evenly.

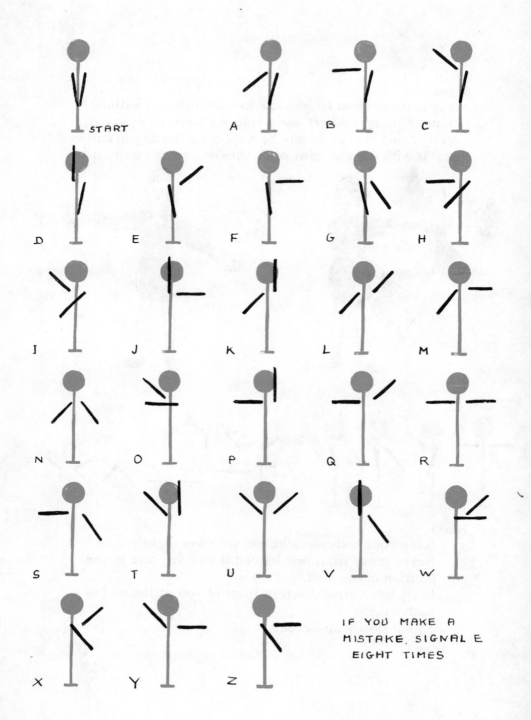

START

A

B

C

D

E

F

G

H

I

J

K

L

M

N

O

P

Q

R

S

T

U

V

W

X

Y

Z

IF YOU MAKE A
MISTAKE, SIGNAL E
EIGHT TIMES

If you enjoy this, try the Signaller Badge.

If you know anyone who can neither hear nor speak, find out if you can help her by learning the manual alphabet.

Bus Time Tables

What do you think of when you see all those hundreds of numbers in a bus time table?

Does it make you feel that you are looking at nightmare arithmetic homework?

OR

Do you realise, that like the compass, these figures or letters are a kind of magic which helps you on picnics, Revels, Pack Holiday and other outings?

The easiest way to understand how a time table works is to look up the buses and places you already know to see how they are arranged. As you grow better at it, pay extra attention to the odd letters and numbers which refer to special notes if you want to be sure of sending your friends off on the right buses at the right time to the right places!

This badge is for the Brownie Highway. It shows the sign for a main road that is used on maps.

(If you enjoy these Challenges, have a look at the Pathfinder Badge on page 161. You may also find there is a link between some of the Challenges on the Brownie Highway and the Pony Rider and Cyclist Badges. See pages 157 and 162.)

Some More Interest Badges

Here are the badges which were mentioned in the Brownie Highway.

Book Lover (A Book)

1. Read six fiction books by different authors and tell the tester about them. You must give the tester a list of the titles two weeks before the test.
2. Make a list of any other books you have enjoyed reading.
3. Show that you know how to cover a new book to keep it clean. Make a bookmark.
4. Show how to use a simple book of reference and the index of a book.

Cook (A Saucepan)

Help at home by doing the following and be ready to do any of it at the test.
1. Make tea and toast. Boil an egg.
2. Cook sausages, bacon, or something similar.
3. Prepare and cook potatoes and one other vegetable.
4. Make scones or small cakes.

Cyclist (A Bicycle Wheel)

1. Own or part own a bicycle of the right size.
2. Keep your bicycle clean and in good working order.
3. Know how to find out lighting up time and why lights are necessary.
4. Go with the tester for a ride showing that you can ride your bicycle safely using the brakes correctly and that you understand
    (*a*) the rules of the road for cyclists.
    (*b*) the signals that cyclists give and observe.
    (*c*) the correct way to turn right at cross roads.
    Note: If you have passed the National Cycling Proficiency Test, you do not have to do clause 4.

Dancer (A Girl Dancing)

1. Do one of the following sections:
    (*a*) *Folk Dance*
        Know three different dances, and be able to perform them really well.
    (*b*) *Modern Educational Dance*
        Make up a simple dance as a character, *or* making a pattern, *or* interpreting a picture.
        (This can be done with or without sound.)
        Perform a simple dance to a rhythm played on a percussion instrument or to a piece of music brought by you.
        Be able to talk to the tester about the dances.
        The tester will be looking to see that you understand the use of your body in space, strong and light movements, and sudden and sustained movements.

(c) *Ballet*

Hold the Grade 1 Certificate of the Royal Academy of Dancing, *or* the British Ballet Organization, *or* the International Dance Teachers' Association, *or* the Imperial Society, *or* any other recognized equivalent.

At the test perform a dance lasting for one minute using the steps in that grade.

(d) *Ballroom*

Select and perform three ballroom dances. Show competence in at least three steps within each dance.

or Hold the Bronze Medal of the International Dance Teachers' Association.

2. Do one of the following:

    (a) Make a scrapbook showing as many different kinds of dancing as possible.

    (b) Know the story of three well-known ballets.

    (c) Choose three countries. Find out about the type of national dancing, the costume worn for it, and the sort of music used for accompaniment.

First Aider (A Cross)

1. Show on a manikin that you can perform artificial respiration by the mouth-to-mouth or mouth-to-nose method. Tell the tester of some accidents following which you might have to give artificial respiration. Know what to do when the patient recovers.

2. Know how to control bleeding and show how you would stop bleeding from the nose.

3. Know how to treat burns and scalds.

4. Show how you would clean around and put a dressing on a grazed knee and cut finger.

Throughout the test you must show how you will reassure the patient and make her comfortable, and that you understand the importance of obtaining adult help.

Hostess (A Cup and Saucer)

1. Show the tester letters you have written:
    (*a*) inviting a friend to tea.
    (*b*) saying thank you for a visit.
    (*c*) accepting an invitation.
2. Welcome and look after a guest or guests either in your own home or at a party, or at a Brownie event. Prepare at least some of the refreshments yourself, and make a flower arrangement to place on the table or tray.

Jester (A Jester's Head)

Either alone or with a few other Brownies entertain an audience in three of the following ways:
    (*a*) Recite a poem. Your choice of poem will be taken into account.
    (*b*) Dress up and act, or mime, or use puppets, to illustrate a well-known story or an event from history.
    (*c*) Make up a dance to a piece of music.
    (*d*) Sing with or without accompaniment.
    (*e*) Dance a national dance.
    (*f*) Play a piece on a musical instrument.

Musician (Treble Clef)

1. On an instrument of your own choice
    (*a*) Play one verse of 'God Save the Queen' well enough to accompany the Pack.
    (*b*) Play two contrasting pieces you enjoy. If you are playing them on the recorder the tunes should cover at least an octave of notes and include F sharp or B flat.
    Tell the tester why you enjoy these pieces.

    or

    (*a*) Sing one verse of 'God Save the Queen' or of your favourite hymn, or a religious song of your own choice.
    (*b*) Sing two songs you have chosen yourself because you enjoy them. One of these must be a folk song of the British Isles. The tester will be interested to know why you enjoy these songs.
2. Satisfy the tester that you can read music by doing a simple piece of sight reading.
3. Take a piece of music to the test and tell the tester what story you can hear in it.

    or

    Make a scrapbook about the life of a composer or musician.

 Music Lover (A Girl Listening)

1. Make an instrument and show how to use it.
2. Draw, trace or collect pictures of instruments of the orchestra and name them.

    or

Make a small collection of pictures of instruments of other lands, and tell the tester what they are.

3. Be prepared to tell the tester about the instrumental families of the orchestra, and by listening to some music be able to pick out one of each family.

4. Tell the tester about any piece of music which you have heard on television, radio, record, tape or at a concert, that has interested you. Take the record or cassette to the test with you if you like.

 Pathfinder (An Arrow)

From your own home or your Pack meeting place:

1. *Town Brownies*   Know the easiest and quickest way you can get to the Town Hall and the best way to get to two nearby towns.

   Country Brownies   Know which road leads to the nearest big town and how far away it is; and the best way to get to three nearby towns or villages.

2. Be able to give clear directions, politely and distinctly to a person asking the way to any of these places: police station; chemist's shop; hospital; telephone; post office; garage; filling station; the nearest doctor.

   Know the days when your local shops are closed.

3. Visit any interesting place in your neighbourhood (church, castle, abbey, battlefield, etc.) and be able to tell the tester about it.

To do this badge you may need to know about bus or train services, so be ready to explain these to the tester.

Pony Rider (A Horseshoe)

1. Catch a pony and put on a head collar or rope halter; lead a pony in hand.
2. Mount and dismount correctly.
3. Ride without a leading rein.
4. Know how to ride along and across a road, and how to say 'thank you' while mounted.
5. Know something about the care and feeding of a pony off grass.

Note: If you hold Certificate D of the Pony Club of Great Britain you can have your Brownie Pony Rider Badge.

Pony Rider (Handicapped Brownies only)

1. Tell the tester:
    how to approach and handle a pony correctly;
    how to catch a pony and put a headcollar on; and
    how to lead a pony in hand.
2. Tell the tester how to mount and dismount correctly. Be able to sit happily and relaxedly, maintaining a correct position at halt, walk, and changes of direction. Hold the reins correctly.
3. Ride without a leading rein, if permitted.
4. Know how to ride along and across a road and how to say 'Thank you' while mounted.
5. Know something about the care and feeding of a pony off grass.
    Know the correct way of giving an apple or carrot, and when to give titbits.
    Know how and where to pat a pony.
6. Name simple parts of a pony.
    Name simple parts of a saddle and bridle.

Safety in the Home (A Fireguard)

1. (a) Tell the tester the telephone number of your family doctor.
   (b) Be able to use a telephone.
   (c) Be able to give directions to the nearest telephone if there is not one in your own house.
   (d) Know how to call the police, an ambulance, the fire brigade.
2. Show how you would do the following in a safe way:
   (a) place saucepans on a cooker.
   (b) wash and dry knives, carry them and pass them to another person.
   (c) strike a match, light a candle and put the matches away.
3. Know what dangers there could be when you use electricity and gas and oil heaters.
4. Explain three ways used in your home to make sure that accidents do not happen.
5. Know how the following can be a danger to young children:
   (a) plastic bags.
   (b) pills and medicines left within reach.
   (c) sharp scissors, needles, etc.
   (d) disinfectants, detergents and insecticides.

Signaller (Semaphore Flags)

1. Out of talking range, send and read short messages in semaphore or morse.
2. Know the following procedure signals:
   calling up (sender), go ahead (reader), I have the word (reader), end of message (sender), message received (reader).
   If you make a mistake: erase (sender), answered by C (reader).

 Skater (A Girl Skating)

To gain your Brownie Skater Badge, on ice or rollers, you must pass Grades 1 to 6 of the Elementary Tests of the National Skating Association of Great Britain.
Note: You can get a copy of these tests by writing to National Skating Association of Great Britain, Charterhouse, Charterhouse Square, London EC1M 6AT. Send them a stamped envelope addressed to yourself, which measures at least 23 cm. × 10 cm.

 Swimmer (A Frog)

1. Swim 25 metres breast stroke or crawl.
2. Pick up an object e.g. a plate, from 1 metre of water; or mushroom float with your face under water for 5 seconds.

164

3. Tread water for 1 minute or float motionless for 30 seconds (not necessarily horizontally).
4. Swim 15 metres on your back.
5. From board, bank or boat perform a standing dive.

Swimmer (Handicapped Brownies only)

1. Enter the water unaided.
    (*Note*: You may be helped to the edge of the water.)
2. Swim 25 metres.
3. Pass one of the following clauses:
    (*a*) Pick up an object from a depth of not less than 1 metre.
    (*b*) Mushroom float with your face under water for three seconds.
    (*c*) Rolling, make one complete turn in each direction.
    Note: After each of the above clauses recover to safe breathing position, upright or floating.

Writer (A Pen and Scroll)

1. Take to the test a story you have written on a subject agreed with the tester.
2. Write an interesting account of an event you have enjoyed as a Brownie, as though you were telling it to someone who would have loved to have been there.
3. Write a letter saying 'Thank you' for a present or a visit or an outing you have enjoyed, and address the envelope.
    Show the tester anything that you have enjoyed writing.

Still More About Ventures

If you look at the Highway you will find all kinds of ideas for Ventures. Can you find any which are quite different from those you have already done?

I expect you have joined in several L.A.H. Ventures, especially some connected with your home, but have you had a 'Fun Out-of-Doors' one yet, or a 'Friendly' one? It is easy to work out a 'Keep Fit' one but what about 'Do Your Best'? You have probably helped in one connected with 'Making Things' but have you found one in which you start by being Wide Awake and end by being Wider Awake still?

As well as being Wider Awake you may sometimes need to be Wider *Away* for your Ventures. If so, you and your Guiders may stay away for the night. This is called an overnight venture.

Anyway, keep your eyes and your minds open for new ideas: someone once said that no one knows what the *last* number is . . . there just isn't one . . . and I think it is the same with ideas. There is no last one: the more you think up the more there are still waiting to be thought of!

Think of Others and Ourselves

Brownies try to think of others every day of the year, but there is one day when we think especially of ourselves – that is, of everyone in the World Family of Guiding.

This special day is called 'THINKING DAY' and is on 22nd February. This was the birthday of both Lord Baden-Powell and his wife Olave, Lady Baden-Powell, who was Chief Guide of the world.

On Thinking Day each year, every Brownie, Guide, and Ranger thinks of her sister Brownies, Guides, and Rangers all over the world, prays for them, and wishes them a Guiding 'Happy Birthday'.

Sometimes on Thinking Day we have special meetings,

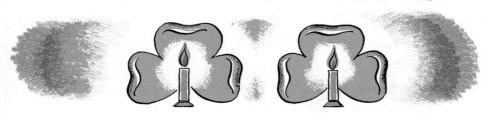

Parties, Services, or Revels, but whatever we do, we always THINK!

A Thinking Day Prayer
Dear Father, bless all Brownie Packs
throughout the world.
We thank thee that thou canst be a friend
to every Brownie, and that thy wise care
is watching over each one of us always.
Let us make thee our very best friend,
now and through all our lives.
Amen.

K. KIRK

Going Up to Guides

The twenty-second of February is a special Guide birth-day when we think of all the Brownies, Guides, and Rangers in the world.

Your tenth birthday is a special day when you think about your own Guide Company which you are about to join.

What are you going to take with you to the Company? Here are some of the things that I expect you will take:

Your Promise which has grown since you first made it and which will continue to grow in the Company.

Your Law which will help you to keep the ten laws of the Guides.

Your Motto which will remind you to carry on with helping other people every day.

Your Brownie Trefoil Badge which is a special badge you will wear on your Guide uniform to show you have been a Brownie.

All the things you have learned on your Ventures and Journeys and in Interest Badges.

What do you know about your Company?
I expect that you know by now:
 Many of the Guides
 Where they meet
 The time of their meeting
 The name of their Guider

And I am sure that you also know the most important thing of all – that

THE GUIDES ARE LOOKING FORWARD TO GIVING YOU A BIG WELCOME TO THE COMPANY!

Index